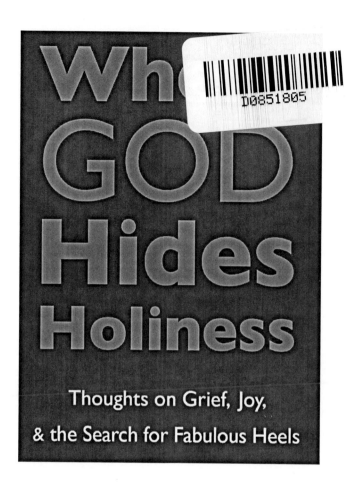

When GOD Hides Holiness

Thoughts on Grief, Joy, & the Search for Fabulous Heels

LAURIE M. BROCK & MARY E. KOPPEL

Morehouse Publishing
NEW YORK · HARRISBURG · DENVER

Unless otherwise noted, the scripture quotations contained herein are from the New Revised Standard Version Bible, copyright © 1989 by the Division of Christian Education of the National Council of Churches of Christ in the U.S.A. Used by permission. All rights reserved.

Morehouse Publishing, 4775 Linglestown Road, Harrisburg, PA 17112

Morehouse Publishing, 445 Fifth Avenue, New York, NY 10016

Morehouse Publishing is an imprint of Church Publishing Incorporated.

www.churchpublishing.org

Lyrics from "The Color of Roses" on page 69
copyright © Beth Nielsen Chapman and Matt Rollings.
Used by permission.

Cover design by Laurie Klein Westhafer

Typeset by Denise Hoff

Library of Congress Cataloging-in-Publication Data

A catalog record of this title is available from the Library of Congress.

ISBN-13: 978-0-8192-2818-5 (pbk.)
ISBN-13: 978-0-8192-2819-2 (ebook)
Printed in the United States of America

Contents

Part 2

Laurie's Story

Introduction

W E ARE BEAUTIFUL MESSES, WE two women. On a good day.

On other days, we are just messes.

Are you a mess too? Maybe? Sometimes? We thought we weren't.

We thought we weren't beautiful messes for decades. Not really. We may have said we understood our messiness and our brokenness, but it was mostly an acceptable answer lived in tidy, well-contained lives. Our lives looked good on paper. Young ordained women in large, prestigious churches. Degrees earned from good schools. Membership in the right organizations. Successful husband. Charming boyfriend. And snazzy shoes. If you saw us from a distance, we looked completely well-appointed and elegant and together. And we were in love with our lives in the church.

Until the church broke our hearts. Until life introduced us to grief and disappointment that stripped us of laughter. Until God reminded us that we were beautiful messes, and we said, "Oh no we aren't. We're priests."

And God said, "Oh, I know. And you're beautiful messes."

We still said no. Being honest about our messiness is hard. So very, very hard. Taking a physics test when the questions are in ancient Greek hard. Seeing the reflection of ourselves with our mess was painful when we first started to look. We wanted to go

■ 1 ■

back, to pretend to be perfect, to be put together again in just that way, but we couldn't.

At first we didn't think the mess was beautiful. We were ashamed of our pain and grief, of the mistakes we'd made and the situations we found ourselves in. We blamed and looked for easy, quick fixes. We found none. But we kept discovering, and after many tears and moments of deep darkness when we thought the darkness had indeed overcome the light, we saw the faintest light of God shining through the cracks. We found the holiness in the mud, and we learned to pray in the ashes. We named our grief aloud. We picked our sorrow up in our hands and touched it to our cheeks. We saw our brokenness as God sees it, not shameful at all, but our tangible, earthy humanness that was raw material in beauty and ugliness, elegance and messiness.

Poet Theodore Roethke says in his poem *The Waking*, "I learn by going where I have to go."

Where we two had to go, we two women, was a path of pain, disappointment, grief, and betrayal that began to strip us of our tidy and well-contained lives. Between us, we experienced three deaths, six miscarriages, a divorce, a failed adoption, abuse at work, and two questionable relationships. And when we needed to grieve, fall apart, and be loved for the messes we are, the place we thought would love us in our messiness, the church, did not. And we realized we didn't love ourselves in our messiness.

The church, or our experience of it during that time, only liked us if we were beautiful.

"But we are priests . . ." we whispered.

And God said, "I know."

This is our story of going where we had to go, for whatever reasons, as we journeyed into our broken souls. These are our words and our truth of dropping into grief and feeling quite certain weeping will not only spend the night, but has moved in as the new permanent roommate. And these are our moments where, in the depths, we found something that amazed us. Our beautiful messes.

Our hope is that as you read our stories, you will touch your beautiful mess in its grief and sorrow, in your heartbreak or addiction or whatever place you have gone that feels so very alone. This is our truth, our pain, our death, and our resurrection. Maybe part of our truth will also be yours. Grief, brokenness, disappointment, and shame are not so original. Yet they are wholly individual. We each walk where we have to go in our own time and in our own way.

This is simply our story of going where we had to go to learn, so that we could eventually look at ourselves and say, "We are beautiful messes, and we kind of love that about ourselves."

And God says, "I know. Finally."

Part 1

Mary's Story

1

Almost Dying
Sucks . . . Joy

"**Y**OU ARE GOING TO DIE," the doctor paused way too long between the two clauses, "if you do not have surgery today." I knew something was up, when in the middle of my ultrasound the doctor called for another doctor to consult. You never want someone to call in a consultant because it means that the news you are about to receive is going to be expensive and dire.

I remember swallowing hard and feeling the plastic clergy collar around my throat. I looked at the doctor, a serious looking woman. She could not have spoken more clearly, but I still asked: "What?" I was supposed to have this baby. Nothing was supposed to be wrong with me.

Only a few weeks earlier, after months and months of infertility, and a little help from Clomid, I discovered I was pregnant. My husband and I were thrilled. At long last, our dream to be parents was coming true.

Soon, though, complications arose. A pain stabbed my right abdomen on and off for those weeks. I would call the doctor's office, but the voice on the other end would coo and reassure me that I was crazy. When I was unable to pee, I sort of realized that maybe I was not so crazy. After an agonizing evening, a visit to the emergency room and close encounter with a catheter, I was in stirrups at the doctor's office watching the doctor get really quiet and call in a consulting physician.

I craned my neck to see the ultrasound screen. A little heart beat on the monitor. That was my baby, and something was wrong because the doctor called for another physician. She allowed me to dress, and delivered her news. She shoved a form under my nose stating that the patient chose to terminate her pregnancy. I had to kill my baby so I would not die. Why did I have to sign this form? No, no, no, no! I burst into tears. I wanted my baby. Just let me die. Just let me die.

Though I did not want surgery, I would have surgery that day. The nurse asked if I had eaten and if so, what. I told her that I ate a Big Mac, fries, and a chocolate milkshake for breakfast (I had been very hungry that morning). Everyone in the room looked at me with shock. Apparently, surgeons frown on performing surgery on people with filled stomachs, really, really full stomachs. What an inconvenience for them!

I made my way out of the examining room to the entrance of the hospital. A nurse accompanied me, I guess because at any moment my fallopian tube was going to blow. She would have to fling herself on top of me, in order to protect the other patients. She looked at me, trying to make small talk, "So, you are a minister?" I nodded and tried to smile. I was not quite in the mood for small talk.

The morning crept into afternoon. Finally the medical staff rolled me into surgery about eight or nine o'clock that night. All the time waiting, I kept wondering if maybe a miracle was coming. Perhaps, this was a mistake. Maybe I would finally wake up.

I did wake up, the next morning, and I knew immediately that

I was empty. I felt so empty. This was not supposed to happen to me. I was supposed to have a baby. I wanted a baby.

The next few days were a sad, sleepy blur. As evening would come, and I crawled into bed, I would cry until I would fall asleep. I just wanted that baby. I wished I had died with my baby.

I never knew that I wanted something so badly. I never knew how empty my life was up until that point, but lying in my bed, trying to recover, I could feel hollowness in myself. How could I feel like something was missing from my life when it never actually was in my life before? How could I miss something or someone I never met or actually knew or held?

Something was missing. Something had been missing for a long time, but what was it? Certainly, my baby was dead and gone, but there was something else missing. My joy was missing. The tubal pregnancy sucked the joy from me, my husband pointed out.

The image stuck with me. Had my joy been sucked out? Was I always to be without joy? Where did that leave me? What was left of me? What did that make me? Was I joyless?

A frightening place to be is wondering how you might replace your joy. One might say that you can become a joy vampire— sucking the joy from any unsuspecting situation or person for that matter. I would not say that I was a joy vampire, but what vampire tells you he or she is a vampire? The joy vampire might just tell you he or she is hungry!

A joy vampire is hungry, so hungry for release from the prison of joylessness, so hungry for joy. You look for joy in all sorts of places, good places and bad places. Unfortunately, as any vampire will tell you, what you sucked, starts to suck. This particular vampire sucked joy from work.

I would go to work and spend as much time at the church as I could. I avoided going home by going to evening meetings. I thought that I was doing something good. I loved that people said that I was so available. I would suck in their adulation, but at the same time I was drained when I returned home to my husband.

For a little bit, I would feel better, but deep down I knew that the need to feed would emerge. I would outrun or attempt to outrun how I felt, but I knew something was coming. Something or someone is always coming for the undead, Death. At any point, the vampire can be confronted with the crucifix, garlic, a stake through the heart, or the light of day. Any one of those instruments causes excruciating death for a vampire, but they also offer the vampire release from his or her undead prison.

No vampire goes looking for death. No joy vampire looks to confront his or her true emotions and fears. No one wants to confront the inevitable and inescapable death. No one wants to look death square in the eye, even if that death is emotional or spiritual. We want to run around like vampires.

We would rather run around like a joy vampire or spiritual vampire because what will happen when our joy or love or hope dies? What will happen to us if or when a joy or love or hope dies? Will we be a coffin, toxic to life?

I certainly felt like a coffin. I felt like my body betrayed me, and that my very soul caused my baby, my joy, to die. I was toxic to new life within me. Maybe I was dying too. Maybe my soul was dying. What would be left of me without that joy, love, or hope? Would there ever be joy, love, or hope again? I did not want to find out.

I wanted to suck the marrow out of the bone, to live! I wanted to feel joy again. I wanted to reach out and grab what I could. Yet, with all this grappling, like a vampire, I still felt like the undead, on the surface, looking alive, but cold inside. In the bright sun of day, lying in that bed, I was empty. My baby was dead. My joy was dead. I hurt.

My joy was dead and all I could do was hurt. Cut off from anything good, from God, I felt like Job: "If I go forward, he is not there; or backward, I cannot perceive him; on the left he hides, and I cannot behold him; I turn to the right, but I cannot see him" (Job 23:8–9). All I had were questions and hurt. Now what?

What do you do when your joy/love/hope dies? What are your choices? Are there any viable choices? Is it any wonder that we fight tooth and nail to hold on to our undead dreams when you see the alternative? Is it any wonder that you start to suck joy? Sure, I believe in the resurrection, but this dying was killing me! Dying was terrifying. Would resurrection, love really come again? I would have to wait and see.

2

Going Home

"I JUST WANT TO GO HOME." I noticed the voice in my head after the tubal pregnancy. It spoke softly. "I just want to go home." I did not speak the words aloud. I did not want to say them in front of my husband, nor anyone else. If I said those words out loud, they would become more powerful.

Already the words would pop into my mind as I drove around the island on visits to my parishioners, after church on Sunday morning, and as I would walk the dog to Baby Beach in the evening. I wanted to go home, but how could I?

Home meant New Orleans, Uptown, the familiar neighborhood of my youth, with its particular rules to life, but how could I possibly go home? My husband's and my New Orleans home had flooded, as had most of New Orleans during the aftermath of Katrina. My husband was taking the bar exam again. We were living in paradise on the beautiful island of Kauai with the kindest and most beautiful people in the world as parishioners. I was finally the rector of a church (that is, the senior priest on a church staff), in Hawaii! We were living the dream, but whose dream was it?

I was unhappy. I missed New Orleans, and somehow I did not

seem to fit in paradise. I wondered if I could just hang on a little longer, perhaps my feelings would change. Then the phone rang.

"Hi, Mary, it is the bishop. How are you?" The bishop of Hawaii was calling. How did he know? How did he sense that I needed to talk?

I started talking, and he listened. I told him my plan. I was going to hang on, tough it out. He spoke softly into the phone: "Mary, I think that you need to listen to what God is telling you. You are unhappy. Your husband is unhappy. You need to leave, and you need to leave soon."

His words were a release for me, and my husband and I began our return to Louisiana. The voice in my head seemed appeased for the moment, and I convinced myself that the return would guarantee that I would reach all of the goals I set out for myself.

I had a plan. I had heard plenty of people quote that old truism that we plan and God laughs, but still I thought I would try. My plan looked something like this: first I would grow up and survive being the youngest child in a wacky family to become a priest. I would become a priest to constant praise and adulation because everybody loves me, and I would love every stinking minute of it! People, my family especially, would respect me. Next, I get married to someone I like and respect. Then, I have children—three in fact. Each one would have a biblical and/or English aristocratic name like Pippen, James, and Eugenia. Finally, I would retire at sixty-five, a jet-setting retired archbishop of Canterbury. I would sip piña coladas and badger anyone who would listen to my war stories as a priest and give my adorable grandchildren candy before I send them home to Eugenia, Pippen, and James, their parents. This is the way things should be! At least this is the way things should have been for me.

This plan was still fully in my mind, when, at age thirty, I returned with my husband to New Orleans. I would find another church to be the rector. We would have our beautiful children. Most importantly I would be able to outrun any sorrow, any grief on familiar ground. I just needed to get home. I wanted to go home.

New Orleans was a strange place to be, just two years after the storm. The streetcars still were not running down St. Charles Avenue, large portions of the city still bore the scars of the storm, and the city seemed empty, maybe not of people, but something was missing. I did not find a position as a rector. Instead I would serve as the third priest on a large staff.

The rector of St. Christopher's Church in New Orleans had called me before I left Hawaii, and asked if I would be interested in the position. I did not hesitate to call him back and say yes. I had some sense that the position was not really where I wanted to serve God in the church, but the position was prestigious and I did not know where I did want to be. I just wanted to get back to Louisiana, and this position made that possible.

The week before I started my new job, I went to a service commemorating Katrina featuring the archbishop of Canterbury and the presiding bishop. From the nosebleed section I saw a young woman walking in the procession, and I wondered who she was.

Laurie and I actually met at my first clergy conference on my return to Louisiana. I eyed her, unsure if I could trust her. She was sassy and really smart. When she walked into the room, she commanded your attention. I was jealous until a mutual friend introduced her to me.

I did not want to like her, but before I knew it, Laurie and I were having monthly chow downs at the Cracker Barrel in Gonzales, Louisiana, a town halfway between our respective cities of New Orleans and Baton Rouge. We would meet and talk for hours about our positions and our lives and our goals. So then she asked the inevitable and obvious question: "So, why did you leave Hawaii?" I was ready for her with a good, well-practiced answer. I put down my fork of mashed potatoes and before I could begin my polished political explanation, she added: "And not the sanitized version."

She knew. Maybe she did not know the exact words, but she knew that whatever bullshit answer I could give might give some compelling reasons for leaving a veritable paradise, but that the true answer was a little less tangible and a little more complicated. So I spoke the words aloud: "I just wanted to come home, and I don't know why exactly, but I was not right there." She did not laugh. She listened.

After that day I knew that God had brought this person into my life for a reason. She would tell me the truth, and I would tell her the truth. When we would talk, I realized what had been missing from my life for a long time—a friend. When I talked with Laurie, the little voice in my head, speaking its mantra, would stop.

3

RESPECT

I SUPPOSE I SHOULD HAVE QUIT my job at St. Christopher's right after my boss's hand made contact with my right cheek, but I was stunned. Two weeks into the new position, my boss, the other priest, and I stood in the mailroom discussing the sacrament of confirmation. My boss spoke about the old tradition of bishop's slapping those who would be confirmed in the face. I asked, "Really?" Then my boss demonstrated, on my face.

The room was quiet as the sexton and the secretary who also saw the slap looked away. I touched my face. The slap did not hurt that much, but something stung. I just remember repeating "You slapped me," surprised that no one seemed to notice or care. That evening I told my husband about the slap and he asked if he should go to work with me the next morning and punch my boss. I laughed and said no, but in hindsight, I should have had my husband go and beat the crap out of my boss.

Strangely, I knew right then that the slap would be emblematic of my whole experience working at St. Christopher's, but I told myself that I needed the position. I was at a large parish, on a large staff in New Orleans. I thought if I wanted to get ahead in the Episcopal Church, I needed to work in a parish like this.

I feel now that there were signs of trouble all around me. My mother says: "On the road to hell, you have a lot of exits. Stop trying to make good time." The slap was the first sign. The next sign came from my husband, who began complaining that I was never home—and indeed, he was right. I was working late every day. I was constantly e-mailing and texting about work, to work, or with people at work when I was home, neglecting or ignoring my husband even. I would complain how busy I was, but I would do nothing to rectify the situation. He began suggesting I quit, but I shrugged off his suggestions.

What did he know? I was working in a large parish, doing exciting things, looking important. The church put on important events, sometimes with important people and big crowds. I was also spending more time at work so I did not have to go home and deal with feeling sad about miscarriages and my marriage. At work, I would constantly try to get my boss's notice and acclaim. I just wanted him to say "good job" or "thank you," but he would never say those words.

Still I was making great time on mama's road to hell until my boss called me into his office one afternoon in early 2010. We talked about an upcoming worship service that our church was responsible for putting together. He wanted to make sure that both women and men where represented in the service. He said, "Mary, I want you to lead this service because none of those other women know what they are doing." He laughed when he said it. I laughed too because I wanted to join in the joke even if it was at my expense as a woman.

That evening I spoke to Laurie on the phone. I told her the exchange. I was bothered, but I was not sure why. She was quiet, and then said, "I think that you are bothered because he insulted you and you went along with it. He does not respect you."

I called my boss that evening and spoke to him about our earlier conversation. He said he was making a joke, not a very good one, but a joke. He assured me that he had the utmost affection for me. I then asked, "Do you respect me?" He hemmed and hawed, but I knew the answer. I had known the answer for three years.

For three years since that slap I had been trying to gain respect from my boss. I tried to gain his approval. Somehow, I think I believed that if I had that approval, that respect, it meant that those disappointments before and during that time would somehow be wiped away.

I talked to Laurie again, wondering why I wanted his respect so badly. She asked me, "Do you respect him?" I answered her immediately: "No way." Laurie sighed, so I knew what she had to say was going to sting a little bit: "Then why do you care what he thinks? And why the hell are you working for him?"

Why was I working for someone who did not respect me, and, more importantly, whom I did not respect? Moreover, was I putting my priesthood, my vocation at risk working for someone I did not respect merely because I wanted the prestige of working at a big parish? How was I going to explain that one to Jesus?

Why had I taken this position? The answer goes back to the voice whispering in my head: "I want to go home." After Katrina, after the first two miscarriages, after leaving Hawaii, and after watching my marriage start to implode, nothing made sense anymore. My life was not supposed to look like this.

When I had fantasized from my perch in Hawaii about coming home, I thought returning to Louisiana would help me understand why these bad things—Katrina, the pregnancy loss, and the attendant strains on my marriage—were happening to me. Really, I thought that somehow coming back to New Orleans would work some magic and suddenly my life would once again follow the trajectory I chose for myself (or thought that I chose for myself).

In New Orleans, I could once again be the youngest child, the McGehee School Girl, the politician's daughter. When I was a child in New Orleans, I was a good girl. I behaved myself and obeyed my parents, siblings, and anyone else who I thought I should please. I wanted to keep the peace and make people happy.

I wanted to avoid conflict and disagreement in a family that was usually filled with argument and conflict. I believed that pleasing other people was my purpose.

I would do whatever everyone else told me to do, and everything would be better. I just needed to follow the rules, but somehow these rules did not seem to work or make sense. I tried pleasing and bending, but I did not feel better. Others' advice now rang false, and just as Katrina has torn the façade off so many structures in New Orleans, these storms in my life were tearing off the preconceived, unquestioned received notions in my life.

I thought the rules were that if you are a good and kind person, people will like and respect you. If they do not like and respect you, just try harder. I thought that the rules were when bad things happen just keep moving because you do not want to be a whiner. No matter what, endure because, well, that is the way life is.

The situation with my boss in New Orleans did not compute with my rules. My boss did not respect me no matter how hard I tried or what I endured. I did not respect him. The question hung in the air around me: did I respect myself? I listened for the voice. This time the mantra changed: "You need to come home," but what did that mean?

I needed to come home, but not to a place. I needed to come home to myself and discover just what respecting myself might mean. First, though, I needed to figure out just who I was.

4

The Dark Night of the Soul is Not Romantic at All

"NIGHTTIME IS THE HARDEST." Two friends, years apart, have said this to me over and over. The first time I heard it, I did not quite understand. My friend spoke about her loss and how she was working through her grief. I would listen, but I did not quite understand what she meant. Only a little time later, I would.

Indeed, nighttime is the hardest when you are hurt and broken from loss. Night is quiet. The house is dark, and it feels empty. For me, I just wanted to fall immediately asleep, but the world of dreams eluded me. I was not afraid exactly. I felt so utterly alone.

I remember while recovering from the tubal pregnancy, I would lie in my bed. On that first day, I napped and rested, but when night came, I felt restless and frightened. My husband had to leave suddenly that evening. His father was dying back in Mississippi. My mother was flying to Hawaii to be with me. I was alone.

It is at nighttime that you really feel it. You are alone. Then the tears come. For me, the wails came out like jagged breaths. Sometimes I would actually make a sound, but what was the point really? Who hears me crying? I would lie there, in the dark, with my pillow getting wet, waiting for the release and relief of sleep. Is this what my friend was talking about? Is this just me? Am I alone in feeling this way at night?

I thought that it was just me, but apparently, this is fairly common. Everyone I have ever talked to about their grief has told me the same thing. Night is the hardest time.

During the day you are okay. When the loss first happens, you cry and wail. You talk to your friends, families, coworkers, anyone who will listen. People are sympathetic for a time. Soon, though, you realize that people start to find your grief distasteful. Something within you stops talking about it as much.

You start to feel better or at least you start to act like you feel better. You know the saying: "Fake it 'til you make it!" You start smiling again. You start back to work or activities that you did before the grief event. Little by little, day by day, people stop asking about you. Life moves forward during the day. There are people and places and activities and so many other things to distract you. But not at night.

At night everything slows down. It slows down just as much as you do. So you can remember and really feel that emptiness and brokenness. I doubt in the dark. I hate feeling that doubt.

I found myself dreading the dark, not because of the fear of monsters, but maybe because a lack of monsters. Maybe if there were a few monsters, I could fight them and pass out. Perhaps I could win them over, and we could have tea together until sunrise. No, in the dark, I was alone again. I was reminded that I was alone.

Scholars and theologians talk about St. John of the Cross's "dark night of the soul." I remember studying him in my Spanish classes, where we knew him as San Juan de la Cruz. We would learn about the process the soul took in its journey to its lover

God. The image sounded so romantic and tidy. Frankly, I still cannot find the connection between the sexy "Canciones Entre el alma y el esposo" ("Songs between the Soul and Her Husband") and the utter desperation you feel wondering if God has abandoned you at your very lowest point. Somehow, lying in the dark, feeling that you are utterly alone is not romantic at all. Staring at the ceiling and crying on your pillow is also very messy.

I wondered how it could be that during the day I could be so sure, and at night, I felt so sad. I talked to my friend about this. She smiled at me and said, "During the day, we can deny how we are feeling because we are around others who are uncomfortable with our grief. Their discomfort makes us uncomfortable with our grief, so we put it away, but it comes back when we have some privacy. It always comes back." Yikes, that sounded like a warning from a Steven King movie. Would I always be crying at night, wondering and wrestling with the loneliness? She seemed so strong in her faith. Was she still crying? She smiled again and said, "It depends."

It depends on whether or not we are willing to go through that "dark night of the soul." Every one of us will be confronted with grief at some point in our lives, and yet we can feel so uncomfortable when we witness grief or exhibit grief. We try to numb the grief with alcohol, drugs, food, or sex. You name it, we try to use it to numb our grief.

We try to avoid our grief with busy work. We try to talk the grief away, dismiss it, or not talk about the grief at all. The grief embarrasses us. We should be happy all the time, at least that is what the magazines say. Everyone else is so happy, so why aren't we happy? So we keep busy, keep distracted, and keep drunk. But you have to sleep sometime.

I had to sleep sometime. Time would once again slow down, and I would lie there with my grief. I wonder when the nights got better. When did I feel less alone? Surprisingly the nights did get better, like the cheesy song says. I guess my evenings improved when I admitted to my old friend about those dark nights. I told her about feeling so alone. I told her about talking and crying to God, asking, "why?" I told her about feeling like I heard nothing back. I was so afraid that if I admitted that I was sad, the grief would swallow me whole and kill me. I was scared that if I did not try to avoid or resist my grief, I would lose my faith.

I am sure some St. John of the Cross scholar would laugh if I said that. This is the soul's journey. This was a time of faith development and crisis. That is all well and good, but it was not helping the fact that I was afraid of the dark. What if I entered that dark and never emerged?

My wise friend would smile again. She did not laugh or dismiss me. Looking at her, I realized that maybe if I felt I could not trust my faith and soul, I could trust her experience. She had already taken this nighttime journey a few years before. The grief did not kill her, and grief would not kill me. The dark would not overtake me. I would not lose my faith.

As time went on, nighttime got easier. I would cry and then pray and I usually fell asleep quickly. I stopped resisting my grief. The questions would come. The tears would pour out. I would ask, "why, why, why?"

I am not sure that you totally get over grief, but I do think that you move through it. It becomes a little part of you, not taking up too much space. It becomes part of your story, but not a dominating theme, just a small detail in character development; just a few hours in the dark.

A few years ago, another friend admitted the same thing to me: "Nighttime is the hardest." I smiled at him and said, "I know." I knew what he meant, and he was not alone in dark. I could be with him taking that long soul journey to God, together.

5

Six

I HAVE EXPERIENCED PREGNANCY LOSS SIX times. Six miscarriages are astounding to me. I sometimes cannot believe that these losses have happened. I am not sure who really knows about what happened to me and my husband. Sometimes I felt like people could see the insurmountable grief etched into my face. Did they notice the passion that is missing from my eyes? I do not know.

My heartbreak might not be evident on the outside, but it was there inside me. I had so much anger, so much grief, and so much sorrow within me that I did not know what to do with it. Sometimes I wanted to cry (okay, I wanted to cry a lot), but I did not feel like I could. Somehow, I was not allowed to express my hurt. I did not want people to see me cry. I was embarrassed by it, I guess. Yet I knew that I had to express this pain if I wanted to do anything because at that time, I was in limbo.

I was in limbo, with the dead, unbaptized babies. My passion was frozen. Have you ever seen a child fall down and for a moment he or she is stunned? Suddenly the pain comes, and the child begins to wail. I was stunned. I was numb and about to enter a world of hurt.

I look at that number six and wonder how stupid I had to be. I felt foolish and stupid. Why, for the love of God, did we try again? I could have kicked myself, but we wanted to have children. We did not set out to hurt ourselves with loss because we did not expect to lose.

People would make kind but utterly stupid comments. I would respond with, "Yes, I am sure that your niece's aunt's hairdresser experienced a miscarriage and now she is the mother of five" and a meaningful nod. I tried to listen respectfully to people's stories, but inside I was torn between anger and crazy hope and wonder. I did not want to hear about this other woman's successful pregnancy and motherhood. I wanted to be able to tell about my successful pregnancy and motherhood. Why did this other person's pregnancy work out? Why not me?

After the person would tell his or her inspiring (sometimes improbable) story, I would tell them that I had lost six pregnancies. Most people usually shut up, but some continued to ask questions. I did not mind answering some questions because at least for a little while I could talk about what had happened. Other times, though, I hated answering the intrusive, seemingly obvious questions: Did we see a fertility expert? Yes, we have gone to a fertility expert. I am a freaking miracle of modern science. I just seem to lose pregnancies for no apparent reason. They cannot explain the why. Maybe we could try again because you know someone who tried again? Yes, I am sure your daughter-in-law went through that too. Uh huh, uh huh, sure. I have heard these stories now six times. Enough already! Let's just say that this is really horrible.

This situation is really horrible and awful and terrible, tragic even. I felt horrible and out of control. I would go through those lousy stages of grief. I knew each step or stage was coming; I could not control or stop them. I would listen to U2's song "One" over and over again in the car and cry. I did that once in front of my husband, and he turned off the radio, so I would cry in secret.

I had no idea how my husband was doing, and I was not sure

how or if I could comfort him anyway. Frankly, I did not care how he felt. Sometimes I thought that I was holding it together, but then I felt I just might start throwing my shoes and writhing on the floor. I am still thinking about doing that. I am still thinking about it.

I guess all I could really do was cry. I cried for what might have been. I cried for what was. I cried for what could not be. I listened for the voice of God. I listened for some purpose in this disappointment and sorrow. I do believe that there was a purpose, but I did not know what the purpose of this loss was. I would cling to the Rock of My Salvation even as I felt crushed beneath it.

I wanted to say that I was not okay, but sometimes I was okay. I wanted to say that I am finished, but I was not (and still am not) finished either. I am not finished with life, with faith, with love, but right then was not about love.

That time of loss was a time of endurance. I endured and kept walking. Even now, I endure and keep waking up each morning. I endured until I could do everyday tasks again, with joy. Slowly, those tasks did become joyful. I endured until I hoped. Hope was coming, but I was still in sorrow right then. Hope was coming and soon I would hope until I witnessed. I would hope until I witnessed and met my Redeemer face to face.

6

Strong and Faithful, and Broken

"Yes, I am an Episcopal priest," I smiled at the nurse. No need to make the situation any more uncomfortable. Boy, did she look uncomfortable. I needed to let her know it was okay. "It's just that I was so happy, the happiest I feel like I have ever been. That's why it hurts so much now. I thank God that I hurt so much now, you see?"

I think back on what I told the nurse. I wonder why I said what I said at that time. I would not say that I was lying, but at that moment, I felt somehow that I had to say it to her. I needed to seem "strong" and "faithful." I am a priest of God, gosh darn it!

I am a priest of God, and yet, at that moment, I wished I had not worn my clericals that particular day. I just wanted to be some anonymous expectant mother. I wanted to be like anyone else. I wanted to sob and fling myself on the floor of the doctor's office. I wanted to run out the door, daring some orderly to catch me.

Once again, I was to have surgery for the sixth pregnancy loss. I thought that the nurse expected me to be what I thought was "strong and faithful." I may also believe the sentiment. As a

Christian, I know that I am not promised an easy life, but I am promised love, and love hurts sometimes. I am promised joy, but joy often comes with a terrible price.

As I think back on that July day, I realize two things: I had way too high an expectation for the priesthood, and way too low an expectation for my brothers and sisters. Or more specifically, I really wanted to be better than everyone else. Ouch. That hurts.

The not so funny thing about hurt is that it seems to be starting place for the truth. When we hurt, we need to tell the truth. We need help! We need support! We are weak! I never wanted to admit that I was weak. I never wanted to admit that I was so angry. I never wanted to admit how much pain I really felt.

I wanted to remain in control. I wanted to seem cool and confident at all times, but that was a lie. I was really hurting inside, emotionally and physically. I was so angry with God. I wanted to know why. I kept these to myself thinking that I could endure, that I would endure on my own.

I think part of me felt that I did not want to be a burden to others. Part of me wanted to believe that somehow being a priest helped me endure pain easily. Both were untrue. Both were based in some misguided or inverted pride.

I did not want to show pain, but Jesus showed pain. Jesus showed his pain, anger, and disappointment. Was I better than Jesus? I think that I was walking dangerously close to idolatry. My priesthood was becoming an idol.

About six months after the last surgery, during my evaluation with my boss in New Orleans, he said to me, "I think that your miscarriages have made you more approachable." Who knew that miscarriages could be such a valuable ministry tool? I raised an eyebrow to him, and we both laughed while he realized how stupid and insensitive he sounded, but his words made me think. It made me realize that while I thought I was covering my pain really well, I may also have been distancing myself from my community. It took the crushing blows of hurt to start to break down the idol I held in my priesthood.

I did not want to be vulnerable, but in my greatest weakness and vulnerability God was speaking to me and to others. I did not want to be vulnerable, but the wall I built around myself and my priesthood left me feeling isolated. In isolation, I could not learn or grow. In isolation, I was withering and my priesthood was irrelevant.

Would people understand that I was weak? Would others accept me even if I was not perfect? Would I still be able to lead as a priest even if I felt so insecure? Maybe the better question: Would I accept and understand others in their weakness, vulnerability, and less than perfection? Would I be able to lead others when they felt insecure? Of course I answered yes. So then the question remained: Was I less deserving of mercy than they were? No, I deserved mercy too.

When I thought I was being "strong and faithful," I was neither. I was distant, haughty even, and cut off. Maybe "strong and faithful" actually meant one had the strength to be vulnerable and ask for help and the faithfulness to admit doubt and anger.

If I did not want to become like a stone idol, some relic of what was, I needed to tell the truth. I needed to admit that I hurt, and I needed and continue to need help. The truth of our faith is not having the strength to face every obstacle but the knowledge that we are not alone and do not need to be alone in our pain anymore. Everyone is or will hurt at some point, a priest is not above hurt, but perhaps a priest can walk with others in their hurt because he or she knows hurt.

I no longer need to seem strong and faithful. I needed to be strong and faithful to who God called me to be, an imperfect person. I needed to be able to cry and to cry out in anger. I needed to be able to lean on my brothers and sisters when I felt so weak and insecure. Maybe when I can admit to my brokenness, I can truly be healed. Maybe when I can admit to my hurt, anger, sinfulness, and failure, I can truly understand and mean what I say when I pray, "This is my blood shed for you and for many for the forgiveness of sins."

Jesus pours out his blood for me and for you. Jesus pours out himself for us. He is broken to heal our brokenness. We are imperfect, but perfectly acceptable to him. Our vulnerability allows him to enter into our lives and heal our heartbreak. Our vulnerability is why he does what he does. Why would we want to be any other way than how God created us to be? Why would we close off that access to God? Perhaps our weakness is indeed God's strength.

7

To Cope or to Heal

A FEW WEEKS AFTER THE SIXTH miscarriage, my husband and I decided that we should try to adopt a child. Within two weeks, we hurriedly filled out the paperwork to participate in the foster to adopt program. Who knew how easy filling out twenty pages of questions and gathering paperwork could be? I wrote our answers. My husband found our insurance cards and marriage certificate and other vital paperwork. We took the classes and got our fingers printed.

Before the ink could even dry on our foster parent certificate, we got the call. Would we come pick up an infant? Would we be willing to care for her and maybe even adopt her? We took off!

The next three days were exhilarating. After suffering six miscarriages, we rejoiced in finally holding a child in our arms. She was beautiful—a little gassy, but perfect.

My husband and I seemed to have found a reprieve from our tragic existence. We were so kind to each other, laughing about little parent mistakes, fighting over who got to hold her next. The cracks in our marriage seemingly disappeared. I started to realize that I was a mother. This mother part of me was vital and real,

and I was good at it! I was discovering a hidden part of my identity as Mary Koppel.

My husband and I were experiencing joy, real joy in loving on
this little girl. The joy that I thought was totally sucked from me
filled me. I was excited, until the fourth day.

On the fourth day, news came. Her birth mother wanted her
back. We—or, rather I—needed to take her to the visits with her
mother and grandmother each week. My husband could not bring
himself to go. Frankly, who would blame him, but I did as I drove
her to the meetings.

Twenty-one days after she arrived, we handed her over to her
birth mother and grandmother. They offered kind thanks to us
for our care. We walked silently to the car.

I ground my teeth to keep from crying as we drove home. I
wanted to fling myself into his arms, but when I looked into my
husband's eyes I felt such hurt from him. He looked as if I had
hurt him, and perhaps I had.

I so desperately wanted to be a mother, and now I had experienced motherhood and realized it was a part of me. We wanted to
be parents so much. I wondered if we had rushed into the foster to
adopt program, lying to ourselves that we could handle what had
happened. Did he blame me? Because I think somewhere in me, I
blamed him. He was always so reasonable and thought out every
step, but he went along with me in this scheme to adopt. He did
not stop me. He should have stopped us.

I knew it was not his fault actually, but once again, had we
been fools? We let our hopes get raised, but I am not sure that we
could have kept our hopes from raising. I am not sure I could keep
from loving her. I did not want to ask, but would it have better
that we never met that little girl? Strangely, the answer was no.

The following Sunday morning we sat on the front porch
drinking coffee before I left for church. He said, "I don't think that
I believe in God anymore because of this." I sighed and thought
to myself, "I don't think that I want to believe in God anymore

because of this," but I did not say it. Instead, I got in my car and went to the parish as if nothing had happened. Four weeks later I moved out.

I never knew pain like losing that little girl. My whole life I would categorize hurts. What I mean is that when something painful came up, like a death, I would usually ask myself: Is this worse than . . . ? Is this better than . . . ? I guess that was my little way of exerting control over my life, my disappointments.

For example, during college I would compare a disappointment over a break-up or failing a test to the death of my father. I would ask, "Is this situation more painful than the death of my father?" The question would effectively shut down any more whining or belly aching. As one can imagine, no failing test or ex-boyfriend would measure up to the death of one's father on the measuring stick of pain.

I always thought that if I could say that the present situation was less painful than a past situation that I have previously suffered through, I somehow thought that I would be okay. Because I moved through the past hurt, this current pain could be easier to move through.

The truth was that I was avoiding pain at any cost. I thought that minimizing my hurts or disappointments would protect me from feeling. I thought or believed that we just needed to endure because that was life. Well, this pain defied category. This pain broke me open.

I started to feel everything, like being hit by a huge wave, and I was struggling and drowning. My last and only chance to be a mother was gone because she was gone, because I could not get pregnant, and because my marriage was gone. Another wave hit, and more pain surrounded me. I realized that I hated my position and my boss, but I had chosen to go there. I had caused so much of my own pain.

I wondered where God was. I saw my idol of God floating around me. It was my goals, my perfect appearing life, and even my priesthood. I needed help. I needed help from the true God, not my idol.

Help came in the form of Frank. I stepped into his office after a friend suggested to me that I should talk with a therapist. I felt unsure. I wondered how he could help me. I looked around his office and my eyes landed on a little wire figure on his coffee table. The figure was a man inside a little cage. He held the bars of the jail, but right behind the figure, the jail door was open.

The first day I met him, he asked why I was there. I matter-of-factly listed my litany of hurts. He looked thoughtfully at me and asked, "Do you want to cope or do you want to heal?" My answer meant that I ended up talking with him once a week for two years.

Healing meant that I needed to learn to swim in rough waters. Learning to swim meant me telling the stories of my life, and telling the truth. So each week I poured out the pain that was inside me. I would tell him about the great sorrows of my life and the menial disappointments. He would listen to both with the same care and consideration, handling each struggle with gentleness and offering coffee. Through his listening, I felt the healing of God.

8

Grinding Coffee

LIKE I SAID ABOUT THE road to hell, I was on it. My job at St. Christopher's Church was frustrating with the realization that I was not respected. The beautiful baby girl that I thought would be my daughter returned to her mother. My marriage was dissolving officially in six months. So I would head to the coffee shop almost every day.

This was not just any coffee shop. This temple of caffeine contained not only the elixir of the gods, but an old elementary school friend named Sal. I recognized him immediately. He still had that friendly smile and wicked sense of humor. We struck up our friendship just where we had dropped it off twenty or so years ago.

Sal made just about the perfect hot mocha, and when the shop was not busy he would always sit and visit awhile. He seemed to listen so well. Every day I went by for my Sal, I mean mocha, fix. He was always on my mind. We were friends.

Okay, maybe we started as friends, but something seemed to change between us. We would even hang out a little bit. We grabbed lunch every now and then. I realized that I felt more than friendship for him, and our relationship was progressing. One day I let the words slip: "I love you." He smiled and said, "I love you too." This would all have been the beginning of the most romantic movie ever except he had a girlfriend.

We would talk. We would text. We would laugh and flirt, but he had a girlfriend. I had even met her, and she was lovely and kind, but we still talked every day. Maybe on the surface our friendship looked healthy and normal, but underneath I knew that I was lying.

Still, I was making really good time on that road to hell. I texted him one evening. I had a bag of coffee beans. I asked if I could borrow a coffee grinder. Twenty minutes later he was on my front porch, coffee grinder in hand. I invited him in, and he ground my coffee beans.

I related the story to Laurie later with a laugh. Laurie was not laughing, "Mary, he came over to your house and ground your coffee beans? Do you have any idea what that sounds like?" I did not care for her tone, "Well, that is what I am saying. All he did was come over and grind the coffee beans. It sounds dirty, but he actually ground my coffee beans. We have never done anything, ever." Laurie spoke deliberately: "Mary, you can say it was innocent, but he has a girlfriend. What are you doing?"

What was I doing? He had a girlfriend, but we still talked and laughed and drank coffee every day. I did not know what I was doing, but I loved being around him, and yet I knew our relationship was not right. He had said he loved me. I told him that I loved him. BUT HE HAD A GIRLFRIEND!

I thought if I lingered longer maybe they would break up, but nothing seemed to change. He and I would continue to talk all the time. Finally I spoke with him again. I asked if he remembered when we told each other how we felt. He did. I asked, "What should we do about that?" He asked, "Why do we need to do anything?" I nodded.

A week later, he pulled me aside at the coffee shop. Sal asked me to perform his wedding to his girlfriend. I smiled, and quickly walked to the exit. I decided then that maybe I needed to switch coffee shops.

I felt like a fool. I thought back to all we had talked about. That evening I spoke with Laurie, sobbing on her couch. "I thought he was going to leave her," I said, but once I uttered the words, I knew that I had been had. I had been taken in by the tease, the false promise of love. Even worse is that I violated my personal code of honor for Sal in hopes of true love. I felt bad about what I was becoming to try to get what I desired.

I felt like so many promises were broken, but the promises were unspoken, implied but never confirmed. Now, in the aftermath, I was left playing the fool. I had acted dishonorably.

"I was a fool," I whispered. Laurie touched my arm, "Hey, that's my friend you are talking about. You might be a fool, but you were a fool for false hope, and maybe being a fool for hope, even false, is not such a bad thing. Better to be a fool for false hope than a plain fool, am I right?"

We laughed then. "So what do I do?" I asked.

"Tell the truth, Mary. Admit that you acted foolishly and selfishly in pursuit of a highly unsuitable cad, admit that you hurt his girlfriend, whether or not she will ever know, but also admit that you pursued because of love. If you get in good with truth, she will probably introduce you to her hot brother named love, and that love will not be based in false hope or a tease, but in truth."

I agreed, but I still needed a new coffee shop.

9

Divorce

APRIL 23 IS THE DAY that my marriage legally ended. That means that I am divorced. I am a divorcee. That sounds like I should be swilling martinis and sexually harassing a scantily clad pool boy named Pablo. I am not.

I am not jetting off to Tuscany to start a new life. I am not dating a younger, hotter millionaire, having the most incredible sex of my life. I am sitting at work, at my computer, trying to keep from bursting into tears.

In five years, we had six miscarriages, four moves, three different churches, one flooded house, and a failed adoption attempt. One might say that the numbers were stacked against us, but others have been able to withstand such blows and their relationships blossomed. Ours, unfortunately, withered. Why?

We are both good people. My ex-husband is a good, decent man. He treats people with respect and kindness. Why were we unable to make our marriage work? When pain struck, why did we pull apart instead of coming together?

Not every moment was marred with tragedy either. We enjoyed each other's company, talking for hours about politics, food, and movies. We attended festivals and fairs, traveled to Rome,

England, and Mexico City together. We shared similar values and morals, both wishing to be caring parents. He turned me on to morning coffee (for which I will always be grateful). I got him going to church (for which his mother is grateful).

So it was with great sorrow when I moved out of our home that September day. Why? What happened? We had such great expectations for ourselves. I had such high expectations for myself, and I failed. I was supposed to be married forever. I was supposed to stick it out and suck it up and make this marriage work. I was supposed to endure until death. I made vows before God, family, and friends. Somehow, this relationship that started with such promise should turn around. After couple's therapy, we realized that it would not.

Somehow we let so much pain grow in between us that we were overtaken. We did not turn toward each other for help, nor comfort. At times, we even turned against each other. All of our good intentions and expectations for our marriage and each other were not enough to make our marriage work. Little by little, we came to realize that we were not the people that we thought we were. We might have similar goals, similar interests, but we were no longer connected to each other. We were friends, but why wasn't that enough? We are good people, but why wasn't that enough?

More and more, it seems to me that marriage is not about whether you are good enough. Marriage is not a reward for good behavior. Marriage is a gift from God. Marriage is a relationship between two people who love each other. God participates in that relationship whenever those two people love and serve each other. When had my ex-husband and I stopped loving and serving each other? Had God left us? Had God ever been with us?

Yes, I think that God was with us, and I think that God will continue to be with each one of us. Did our marriage not work because we were not good enough? Frankly, I still wonder, if we had just tried harder, would our marriage have worked? At the time, I was so exhausted and hurting that I really did not have any energy to give to our relationship. I wonder, but now I am divorced.

I am a divorcee. That sounds strange to me. I picture wearing a silk robe and turban. I am smoking a cigarette and sipping a cosmopolitan. I sit there making snarky comments to those around me, complaining about the heat of the sun and a lack of good company this year at the shore (not sure which shore that is). Of course I know that is not really me at all. Instead I find myself shooing cats from my front porch, shouting, "I am a divorcee, not a spinster! Beat it, cats! I will not start collecting you!"

Some friends have suggested that I should get out there, get back in the saddle, and live it up. I should celebrate this newfound freedom. Uh, yeah, okay I will do that. Others have said that I need to never think about my ex-husband (that is strange to say as well), and I should hate him. Not really helpful advice either.

I am not sure how one quickly moves on when so much hurt still remains. Probably the greatest hurt from divorce is losing my best friend. I lost my best friend. I think about silly sights and stories all the time that I would love to share with my ex-husband, but we cannot really be friends like that anymore.

For a long time, I did not want to admit how upset I am about being divorced. I did not want anyone to know that I felt doubts and fears about my marriage's demise. I feared that I would hear: "Why didn't you just try harder?" I wanted to be jubilant and excited to be free. I wanted to put on a confident face. I tried to put my spin on a situation that I am still not sure how I got into exactly. I did not want to admit how sad and upset I still am about my divorce because that means I have to admit that I really loved my ex-husband and I hurt him.

Who wants to ever admit that he or she hurts the people that they love? I certainly do not, but through this divorce, I have discovered about myself things I would rather not know. No one wants to see that he or she hurts other people in his or her pursuits, but we do. No one wants to see that he or she is responsible for his or her actions even when in pain, but we are. Once you know these kinds of things about yourself, you feel pretty bad. So what do you do? Well, here I stand, in the need of prayer and forgiveness and a little bit of healing too, if you do not mind.

Like I said, I am not sure how one quickly moves on, but I guess you just do. I am not sure that moving on is just a matter of running out and grabbing the next available man. For me, I need to start forgiving and letting go. I recognize through this divorce that I have learned a lot about myself—who I was, who I am, and who I will be.

I will honor my dead marriage because for better and for worse, it is a part of me. I am who I am because of that marriage and my ex-husband. I will be who I will be because of this divorce. Soon, I am sure my ex-husband will become the ex-husband. Soon, I hope, I will be ready to love and receive love again, with God's help. But for now, I am taking one day at a time, remembering and reflecting on what was, what could have been, but was not, and what will be.

10

Put Her Down

SITTING AT THE KITCHEN TABLE, I looked at my Lord across from me. He was exactly as I imagined him because this is what I imagined. He looked great, red robe over blue tunic, beautiful brown hair and eyes, glowing halo. We needed to talk. He smiled.

"Uh, Jesus, I have been thinking a lot lately, you know . . . " I moved my coffee cup around, trying to swirl the invisible contents.

He smiled and interrupted, "I know, you are thinking a lot about her."

I was thinking a lot about a little girl who had entered my life many months before. She was my foster baby. For twenty-one days, I cared for this newborn girl, like her mother. Hell, I was her mother for those twenty-one days. My ex-husband and I thought that we would be able to adopt her. Instead, she returned to her mother, and all I had was a broken heart and pictures.

After she left, at night, I would call out her name, but I heard no reply. I tried to console myself that she was okay, but I wondered what if she was not. Who was taking care of her, if not me? I did not know what was going on with her, and at the same time, I did not want to know.

"What is happening with her? Is she okay?" He did not answer me. I had no inkling of what might be happening from his expression.

"She is not your responsibility." He said it as a matter of fact. I knew that legally that was true. I knew that my friends and family had said the same thing, but what if? Who was taking care of her? Was her mother doing as good a job as I could have done?

"Her mother is taking care of her. Her mother is responsible for her." I looked up about to object with a "but," but he shook his head. With his head shaking, I knew he was telling me that she was not coming back to me, no matter what kind of mother I was. She was not mine.

"I know that she was not mine, but how am I supposed to let her go? Why do I have to let her go? Why could she not stay with me?" At this point I am pounding my fist on the kitchen table. I think that Jesus has spilled a little coffee on his robe. I look at him apologetically. He just smiles kindly at me. His expression feels like a hug, but he will not answer these questions for me. I guess because these are not really questions. They are my demands.

Jesus looked at me, the way he always does: "Maybe you need to put her down."

I look at him like he is crazy. I cannot put her down. If I do not keep worrying, if I do not keep thinking about her, I am being disloyal. If I stop torturing myself, she might think that I did not love her. At the same time, I never wanted to cause her any pain. I always want her to feel love. I want her to have no interruption in love.

Who am I kidding? I want her back with me. To hell with her mother, I am her mother! I want my baby back! She cannot take care of her like I can. Secretly, I fear that I will never have that love again. I will never have the love I feel for another so strongly that I might stare down death and win. My life will be empty. I will be empty.

"How do you know that?" He knew what I was thinking. Yikes!

How embarrassing! I shrug because he is right. I cannot know for sure that I would be a better mother to my foster baby. I cannot know that I will never feel love for another so completely again.

My Lord speaks again: "You have said that you never would want her to feel that she was not wanted, nor have any lapse in love. You have said that because she is so young, it would be better that she never remember that she was separated from her mother. Do you want to cause her distress?"

I hang my head, shaking no. I cry to think about causing that beautiful girl any pain. Heck, I could barely watch her get her first set of shots without bawling. Still, I wonder, how do I let her go?

"You let her go." I look at him again like he is crazy. Just like that, I am to let her go? I need to keep carrying this hurt. I need to keep this vigil going. What will I have without this hurt?

"No, you need to put her down, she is not yours," I hear him saying this, but I do not understand. I do not want to put her down. I want to keep hurting because it means that I loved. I want to keep hurting because I will be alone without that hurt, I think. I want to keep holding her to me tightly, but she is becoming heavy in my chest.

"You need to put her down, Mary. She does not belong to you. This burden does not belong to you." I know that he is right. I should put down this weight because it sure is heavy.

"But what about me? Will I ever have that love again? Will I ever be a mother? Will I be okay?"

Jesus looks into my eyes: "Do you trust me, baby?" Yes, I do trust him. At least, I say that I trust him, but he has not answered my questions. Or maybe he has answered them. In my mind I decide that if Jesus says that I need to put down this burden, if I need to put down my foster baby, I will put that burden down. I will put her down, but only if he says put her down.

"I am telling you to put it down. It is not yours. Put her down, Mary." I nod. I will put her down, lay her in his arms. I will put down the worry, fear, and anxiety at his feet. I will put down my expectation that she will ever return to me.

"Do you trust me, baby?" Jesus asks me this question again. The way he asks this question reminds me of only a few times in my life when I experienced true trust. I remember standing at the edge of a pool, looking at my mother in the water. Will I jump into her arms? Will she catch me? Well, apparently I did not drown.

Do I trust that Jesus has something else, someone else, some other joy, love, hope for me? Will I walk in faith? Can I wait in expectation of his miracles and grace, when I have felt such pain and sorrow? Is this conversation even real?

"Okay, I will put her down because you say so." I start to cry. I have put her down. I look again at my Lord. He smiles at me, kind of like he has a secret he is going to tell me, but decides instead to keep it to himself.

11

The Miracle of Love Will Take Away Your Pain . . .

THREE MONTHS AFTER MY DIVORCE became final, the call came at 5:30 p.m. on Monday, July 12, 2010, in my office at St. Christopher's Church. My social worker called to tell me that she had my daughter, would I come pick her up? She called her my daughter. I did not have a lot of time to decide. Would I like her or not? I needed to decide now.

In that moment, the world seemed to pass before my eyes. I remembered immediately my previous experience with foster care. I thought of the little girl who returned to her mother. I remembered crying, really sobbing.

I looked around my busy office. I was in the middle of running a summer camp at the church. I had just recently moved into my new place. I did not have a room set up for any child, nor did I have clothing, diapers, food, or a bed. I was not ready or at least I was unprepared, but love does not come when we think that we are prepared. Love and joy come.

I could be hurt again. I could be really, really seriously hurt. I knew that once I got this child, I would not hold anything of myself back from her. I would have to love her completely because I would not be able to stop myself. Right then I had the opportunity to save myself that possible, if not probable heartache.

Should I ask someone else what they thought? No, I knew what I would hear. I should make a prudent, sensible decision. I asked God what he thought. Was this what he was talking about? Do I trust him?

The decision was mine, all mine. My destiny was cradled in my hand, a woman on the other end was clearing her throat. Would I take the child? She needed a decision.

I said yes. As the word slipped from my mouth, I thought I was out of my mind. What would my mother think? How would this work out? How was I going to take care of this little girl? Would she go back too? Would I be hurt again?

I breathed in and out and dialed my mother. The time between getting into the car, picking up my mother, and driving to social services, I remember nothing. I only remember when the worker placed an infant in my arms. She was so small and a little funny looking.

By 6:30 p.m., I held six pounds, two ounces of pure love in my hands. I knew that indeed I would be heartbroken again, but I welcomed the opportunity to love again. When I held my daughter for the first time, I knew she was mine, and I was hers. I knew that I would pick her up and never put her down again.

At the same moment, strangely, I could no longer remember all the details of my miscarriages. I could not remember the hurt of losing the other little girl. I could not remember the hurt of the divorce. Perhaps this was because of sleep deprivation. Or perhaps I have experienced a miracle of love.

There is a great Eurhythmics song with the line: "The miracle of love will take away your pain, in this heartless world, when a miracle of love comes your way again." [1] Over and over again, the scripture speaks of "New Life." Was this what Jesus meant? Did my daughter's new life give me "New Life"? You bet!

How should it be that my joy was wrapped around my daughter's little finger? My joy was no longer my joy. I only knew joy through knowing her, knowing love. My joy was wrapped in the well-being, care of another. Oh crap!

So much of my life I have spent looking for joy and happiness within myself. I have been taught that one must find completion in him or herself. One must be content with him or herself. Well, those theories are all well and good, but my utter contentment, completion, happiness, and joy appear to depend on someone else being near to me, part of my life. I pride myself on being an independent lady, not prone to gushing, but I had no idea how lame I was before.

As a little girl, we used to sing: "I've got that joy, joy, joy down in my heart." Now I know why I have that joy. Now I know why anyone has joy. I have joy because I can love someone else. I can share my life with another. I can give the very best of who I am, what I am in the care of someone else.

I have joy because someone loves me too. Someone needs me and appreciates who and what I am. Someone is glad to receive what I can give of my life and self to her.

I never realized that love could heal. I never realized that love could raise the dead in me. Love raised what was dead in me, my dream to be a mother, my joy in life. Love gave me joy.

At the same time, I also know the possible consequences. I know what happens when joy can leave, when joy is taken away. Am I willing to risk my heart? Am I willing to die for love? Am I willing to die figuratively and literally?

Jesus gives himself to us. He puts himself out there, healing and teaching, suffering and dying. From the outside observer, he

---

1   Annie Lennox and David A. Stewart, "The Miracle of Love," *Revenge*, RCA, 1986.

looked like a failure and fool. But what does that observer know about love?

What did I really know about love? Maybe that is the only way to understand what and who Jesus is. You must know something about love. You must feel love, and also recognize the fear that accompanies love. You can lose so much, so easily. Your well-being, your heart resides in the hands of another. Jesus puts his heart, his life in our hands.

I put my heart in my daughter's tiny hands. She did not smile, nor laugh for those first few weeks of her life. I believed that she would, though. When she finally started looking at me, for me, joy gushed through my heart. When she was able to smile at and to reach for me, the joy poured from every pore of my body.

Is Jesus that mother of us all? Is he holding and caring for us, hoping that we will respond? Does his spirit soar when at last we can blow kisses back to him and give those kisses so freely to everyone we see? I believe he does.

Paul writes that we love because we first were loved. Does God love us as much as I love my daughter? If I am willing to believe that God does, then heaven help us! We are adored, protected, and precious. God will go to the very point of death and beyond for us. What joy! What reckless love!

12

Creating a Crisis

I TALKED MY BOSS AT ST. Christopher's into firing me. I am thinking about the conversation right now. I told him that I was looking at other churches, perhaps hoping to have a new call by the summer. Next thing I know, he tells me that he will announce to the vestry that I will no longer be at the church after June 1. Uh, what?

He says that I quit. I say that he fired me. Perhaps we are both confused. No, scratch that last statement—I am not confused, but maybe he is. The long story short is that I am not working.

My hindsight is incredible. I can see all the way to the beginning of time. I can tell you every stupid thing I said in that meeting that led to this stupid situation. I do have a little (just a tiny bit) of responsibility in this fantastic muck-up. I should never have said anything to my boss about looking elsewhere. On the other hand, we are priests of God, and priests know that we are called one place or another. Priests should be able to speak truthfully with each other. Priesthood is not just a job. Of course, after this fiasco, maybe priesthood is just another job.

Now, after the fact, I am still flabbergasted. I tell some people that this was a well-thought-out decision on my part. I needed time with my child because I never got maternity leave. I use language like "I was feeling called away." Both statements are true. Frankly, I really needed to leave my former position. I was quickly becoming a bitter burnout queen. I did miss spending time with my daughter. I did feel called away (and I did not like working for my former boss). That all being said, I was still fired. Ouch. I like sausage, but I certainly do not like how it is made. I might have needed to leave my former position, but I did not want to leave that way.

My therapist would call what I did in that meeting "creating a crisis." I needed to change. My situation needed to change. I knew early on that my position was not right for me. Why was I working for someone who did not respect me and whom I did not respect? What was I going to do about it? Nobody changes willingly, so sometimes we create a crisis so we will have to act. I created a crisis all right. Now I need to act.

I hate that I was fired. I am so embarrassed. I feel like everyone is looking at me and shaking their heads at my utter stupidity. I really hate to be stupid. I hate having my pride bruised. I feel worthless. How could I have lost my job? Why couldn't I have called in sick that day to work? Why did I say what I did in that meeting? Stupid, stupid, stupid . . .

At other times I shake my fists at the sky, calling down curses on my ex-boss. I ask the voodoo gods to make the elasticity wear out in his socks so they will bunch in his shoes. I try to act as if I did not participate in this fiasco, like I did not have any control over my big mouth. I want to blame everyone else for my actions in this situation. I try to play it cool.

Sometimes, I smile broadly and go on and on about how great having this free time is. I can finally start that novel I have been talking about. I can start losing some weight. While I am at it, maybe I can move to Goa and become a guru to the rich and powerful. This free time is great, I tell you!

Actually, the free time is not all that great, and it ain't free. I am slowly draining my savings. Also, I personally do not need this much "free time." All this time on my hands gives me too much time to think.

I think about what I should have said differently. I was so cavalier when I was talking to my boss that day. I told him the truth that I was looking elsewhere, how I felt, and my difficulties there. I believe in telling the truth, and that is all well and good when you are making money. I ask myself how I will make money. Will I ever get another position?

I start to wonder if I ever made any right decisions in my life. What led up to this point? I then take that painful walk down memory lane. I question: Where is my good judgment? When something did not turn out as planned, was it actually a terrible decision and failure? Where was God in all these decisions?

You look back on your life and wonder that perhaps every decision or lack of decision led to this very moment. God led me here, and this is, well, not exactly where I would like to be. So did God really lead me here or did I take a few wrong turns? Is God even paying attention? Why didn't God warn me?

I start to wonder: Is God still in control here or am I on my own? Did I just mess things up so badly? Was every decision I made before a mistake? My judgment must stink! I thought that I was stepping out on faith, but maybe I was not. When was the last time I made a good decision?

I guess the answer to that question is a matter of perspective. It depends on where you are standing. When you are standing on that high mountain peak, looking back, every step and every slip led you right there. You are surrounded in glorious majesty. When you are standing in the cold, dark valley, with a gash on your leg from a fall, you wonder where you are. You feel alone.

When I was in college, I walked 280 miles of the Road to Santiago de Compostela in northern Spain. Each day, our group would walk between eight and twenty miles through the woods, along roads and up mountains. The only marking for the path were yellow arrows painted on trees or rocks or signs on the side of the road. Many times you could walk for what felt like an eternity before you saw a yellow arrow. In that in-between time, you felt so sure that you might die in the wilderness, and that you were no longer on the path, if there really was a path. You often walk alone for hours, and you feel it. You feel alone.

Right now, I feel alone. I ask myself: What have I done? Will I be living in a van, down by the river? Have I ever done anything right in my life? I wonder what God is doing now. Will I ever get out of this place?

I guess it is a matter of perspective. Indeed I have made some mistakes and made bad decisions. I suppose I could say that I am hurt right now and miserable. My pride is bruised, but I am not utterly lost either. Maybe I need to look around and really see where I am and realize who I am. Do I have perspective at all? Can I see any yellow arrows?

I am quick (and I suspect I am not alone in this) to want to throw my hands up and say that every mistake, every choice I made was terrible when something like this happens. And yet, God can use it. God is using it. Maybe every decision was a mistake, but then God is a God of second chances.

God can take all my stupid judgment calls. God can take all my missteps and still redeem me. God can take all my bad decisions, and God can still teach me. Right now, maybe I am learning humility. I certainly feel humbled. I am also gaining more and more empathy for my other brothers and sisters who are out of work.

It is a funny thing about this unemployment: you start to notice how many other people are in the same boat. As much as I feel I am alone, I look around and see others are in the same place I am. Other people are on this same scary path, looking for reassurance and guidance. When I hear a news story about unemployment, I understand what that feels like and who that looks like. I have a new perspective on an aspect of life I am not sure I ever wanted to have.

My perspective right now might be a little skewed. Right now I question every choice for the last ten years. Not all worked out, but in better times, I would have said that all those decisions helped make me into the person I am. Right now, I might wish that person was employed, but I guess that those decisions did indeed form me.

I suppose, though, that if I had always made the right decision, I would not be all that interesting. There is so much I really would have missed out on. I would not have traveled across the world and met interesting people. I would not have experienced marriage. I would not have become a foster parent and become a mother. It has been in those reckless, faithful moments that when I said "yes" that I believe I really have grown. I am not sure that I really regret my decisions, and I am not sure what good regret really does anyone.

I reject regret. Regret is that Monday morning quarterback always telling you what you should have or could have done, but did not do. That is all well and good, but the last time I checked, no one I know can actually see the future (but if you know someone, give me a call). I reject regret, but I also embrace personal responsibility. I am human, and I make mistakes even when I do not want to admit it, but I need to admit it. Sometimes we need to admit that we make mistakes. Sometimes we need to wonder if we chose wisely, with love and God's guidance or with our own agenda. I think that only if we can admit our mistakes and acknowledge the hurt it causes us, then we can open ourselves to God.

As much as it hurts my human pride, perhaps I had made the wrong choice in talking to my boss. I chose wrong, but I am learning. I chose wrong, but I know that God is using this to make me right. Yes, I needed to leave my old position, but I chose the wrong way to make that move. I acknowledge that I made a mistake, but I need to move on. Right now, my perspective is limited, but soon I will see where each step has and will lead me. I am looking for my yellow arrow.

I hope it points to something wonderful. I hope that I am moving up toward that peak. I want once again to look back on this time and see it in its proper place, a stumble along the journey. I hope that it will help me and others in the future. I hope it is part of the path, but right now I feel a little unsure, unsure of myself and unsure on the path. Is this indeed the faith walk? I certainly hope so.

13

Anger and Free Time

I FELT SO ANGRY AFTER GETTING canned. I was now hustling to find new employment. I was trying to keep my cool in interviews, but no matter how hard I tried, I could not seem to keep down my anger. I wanted to stuff my anger away. I did not want to be an angry person.

Maybe I am not totally comfortable with anger. I used to spend a lot of time around an angry person. I would watch him throw and break things, scream, and curse. After he died, I thought that anger was in my DNA. I feared that if I got angry, the anger would stick.

I tried to avoid getting angry or admitting that I was angry. The anger would then find funny ways to seep out, like shouting a line of expletives upon discovering the store was out of my favorite brand of Hot Fries. I thought that getting angry was somehow ungodly. I guess I thought that Jesus chasing people out of the temple with a whip was a reasoned and well-thought-out reaction to disgust at the wicked practices of the Temple elders. Jesus never got angry, right? Neither should I.

I plastered a smile on my face, but inside I was seething. I was seething with anger at my ex-boss. I was seething with anger at God. Most of all I was seething with anger at myself.

I asked myself why I could not just make my position work. Going deeper, I asked why I could not just follow the rules and expectations I originally held for myself. I would then squash the discussion.

Finally, Frank asked the question I dreaded: "Do you feel angry?" I blurted out the answer: "Yes, but I do not want to." He asked, "Why not?"

Because I was afraid that I would never come back from the depths of anger, like I was afraid that I would never come back from the depths of sadness. I wondered how I could deal with the anger. Frank answered, "You actually deal with your anger; you accept it; you swim in it."

So I started swimming in my anger, realizing it would not overtake me. I felt so angry about not working, but at the same time I was missing that I now had time. I might not have money, but I had time.

With that time, I would work as a substitute priest (when a church's head priest or priests were on vacation) around town on Sunday mornings. As Holy Week and Easter drew closer, and I was still without a church position, I offered my time to a friend at her parish. I would help her with Holy Week and Easter. She needed the extra help.

On Palm Sunday, we handed out portions of the Gospel reading to the different members of the early morning service to read. We stood in a semicircle in front of the chapel altar and read. For the first time in many years while listening to the Passion Narrative, I began to cry.

Later that day, at home in the backyard, I wondered why I was so moved by this particular narration of Jesus' betrayal, torture, death, and burial. There was nothing notable about the reading. James Earl Jones did not suddenly emerge and speak one of the lines. In the past, I have heard the Passion sung perfectly by a choir. I have also heard the Passion read by readers who really knew their parts, but I have never been moved like this before. Random individuals reading parts of Jesus' story in their own voices had touched the grief and anger within me.

For the first time in a long time, I had time to actually listen to the service. I had time to actually feel what I felt. I was so angry about having this time between positions. I was so angry about losing babies, and that little girl. I was so angry about the end of my marriage. With nowhere else to go or be, I had to listen to the Gospel about Jesus' hurt, failure, and sorrow. Listening to his story was allowing me to listen to my own.

I might have felt angry about the time, but I needed the time. Until I actually took the time to deal with my anger, God was going to give me all the time in the world.

14

Getting Yes in a No World

MY FRIEND'S MOTHER SELLS MARY Kay Cosmetics. Technically, she is a Mary Kay director. That means that not only does she sell Mary Kay to any person with skin, she now trains and directs other women in selling Mary Kay. Connie is amazing.

Connie is so amazing she got me wearing sunscreen in high school before sunscreen became cool. She is the only person I purchase skin care and cosmetics from. She has also managed to rope me into being a Mary Kay consultant. The woman has talent. Right now, I also needed a little cash and a lot of confidence.

Part of this consultant gig is training with Connie. I realize that I am not that interested in cosmetics, but I really like and respect her. I like learning from her. In the time we have spent together, learning about selling Mary Kay and building a business, I am learning a lot about life. We live in a world of no.

Lately, I had felt like I am surrounded by the no. I felt like a great failure. My body told me no. My husband told me no. My ex-boss told me no. I might be the Queen of No.

As Connie teaches, we live in a world of no, but in sales, you are trying to get to yes. Through your presentation and pitch, you are trying to convince others that yes, this product is good and good for them; yes, they should buy this product; and yes, they should sell this product too. In sales, you must also know to whom you would like to sell.

People have objections. No, they only buy Clinique. No, they do not have time to hear about this exciting new product. No, they do not have any money.

The world seems to have endless objections. No, you do not belong here. No, you are not pretty enough. No, you are not smart enough. No, you may not get this job. No, your body will not cooperate with you.

At the same time, you are making your pitch. You want to reach out to others with the good news of God's love. You want to give love. You want to receive love. You are trying to overcome the objections that the world places before you.

At Connie's training sessions, she likes to give a sheet about overcoming objections. She does not accept that no is the final word. No might dominate, but her faith in what she is doing and who she is pushes her forward. She keeps asking. I am so impressed with her confidence.

Connie has confidence in what she is doing because she believes in Mary Kay. Connie believes that she has something worthwhile to share with other women. That something is Connie.

She handles rejection with grace and continues to sell, continues to ask. I tend to expect people to say no. I expect the world to say no, so I do not want to even ask.

You would think that by now, through my experiences, I would be used to rejection. I would be used to failure. In fact, I was terrified of receiving another no from someone. I did not want to apply for another position because I immediately assumed a no would come. I was starting to believe that when someone would tell me no or the world tells me no that I did not deserve a yes. Indeed, I am a reject. I am a failure. I will never rise above my fate.

I had this tape playing in my head, paralyzing me. I cannot possibly tell someone about Mary Kay because I just know she will laugh. I cannot possibly send out my resumé one more time because that church does not want me. Through my time with Connie, learning about Mary Kay, I discovered that maybe the biggest no or obstacle I needed to overcome is in my own mind. I was saying no to myself.

Did I believe that I had something to offer this world? Or did I believe the world's assessment of my worth? Did I believe in who I am and what I am doing? Could I see value in myself and what I was doing? Was I living as if I would receive a yes? Was I ready to step out of the tomb? Does the world really get the last word?

No, the world does not get the last word. Connie taught me that even if this is a world of no, we must live like we will receive a yes. Because the real work, the truly hard work comes when we receive the yes.

You see Connie teaches that the hardest part in selling Mary Kay is selling Mary Kay. What I mean is that once you have that initial yes, you have to follow up. You have to meet that wonderful, kind woman and help her find the right skin care and cosmetics. The relationship between consultant and customer begins.

Sure, you thought that no one would buy, but now someone has. She even likes the product probably because she likes and trusts you. You must challenge what the world has taught you about yourself. You are not rejected. You are not worthless and dead. You have to respond to your customer and the world.

When we receive the yes, we need to pay attention. In a world that fosters rejections, in a world that crucifies and buries us, in a world that says no, we can easily believe that we are rejects. We can easily believe that we are worthless and dead. We can sit in that tomb, in that cold, stale cave. When Jesus says yes, can we respond? Are we ready to leave the tomb and leave behind what lies behind us?

Believe it or not, I actually sold about $500 at my first Mary Kay party. I was amazed. Certainly, I like the product, but I had no idea anyone would want to buy it from me. I was surprised by the kindness and interest those who purchased the product showed me. The experience made me question many of my assumptions about myself and the world.

I look to Connie and see that she believes in what she is doing. She loves Mary Kay! She loves what having a small business has done for her. She loves that she is able to help women feel good about themselves through how they look at themselves and take care of their skin. Trust me, if you spend five minutes with Connie, you will feel great about yourself.

Connie also believes in herself. She believes that she will get that yes because she has gotten the yes in the past and she is worth the yes. The no does not deter her from her mission to care for the skin we are in. From Connie's example, I was beginning to realize that I also have worth and am worthy of the yes.

The question truly was did I believe what I said I believed? I said that I believe that God created the world and God loves all of God's creation. God has called the creation good. Jesus gives us life, and Jesus gives us life abundantly. So what does that make me? The world might be telling me no, my brain might be telling me no, but Jesus tells me yes.

Jesus says yes in a world of no. At first, his yes is an unexpected whisper. His yes often comes in unexpected opportunities and relationships. Those yeses call us from the tomb, from the world's assessment of us. Peering from the mouth of the cave, in the light, we finally see what the world should really be and how we can be. The no is not insurmountable. We can overcome the objections. The world does not get the last word on our value.

Fear and doubt might have great press, but neither will have the last word in God's kingdom. When we finally step from the tomb, we know that death and failure and rejection are not to be feared. They are part of the system of the world, but we have overcome the world. We get to live again, and we get to live differently.

So life looks differently on the other side of death. I know the truth, so will I live like I have been resurrected? What do I have to fear when death and fear and rejection are taken out of the equation? How do I live without the no? Or rather how do I live into the yes? I am not sure, but I know that yes means new possibilities and challenges. Yes means seeing myself differently.

I will probably not continue to sell Mary Kay, but I know a great Mary Kay lady, if anyone is interested. The Fancy Nancy lip gloss is awesome, and I love the TimeWise facial cleanser and moisturizer. I will continue to give my pitch to get my yes.

15

At Last

FINALLY, THE PHONE CALL CAME in the late afternoon on a Monday. The woman on the other end offered a position. I got the job! I got a job! After almost a year of unemployment, underemployment, self-employment, after a quick interview, a woman was offering me a position. At the same time, an old friend invited me to visit his church for a position there. What a reversal! Finally a yes!

I had sent resumés. I had submitted to phone interviews. I had talked to different deployment officers around this great country, and I felt like all I was receiving was rejection. I was not working—so I must have done something wrong.

During this time of not working, I cried at night, wondering if my child and I would starve to death under a bridge in a cardboard box. Would I blow through all my saving? Should I do something else? But did I have any skills? What did I know about anything else?

I felt let down by my bishop and diocese. No one seemed to want to help me find a new right position. I felt like the church did not want me to serve as a priest anymore. I wondered why the church was treating me this way. I felt forgotten by my diocese. I was also embarrassed to see anyone lest they ask me what I was doing. What would I tell them? I was hanging out at the local coffee shop during the day, using its Internet to look at positions that I had nothing to offer and had nothing to offer me.

I prayed and railed angrily to God. Why was I going through this? Give me a job, damn you! There was no bright side of this stupid free time being unemployed. I felt miserable, and the rejections just would not quit. I would get e-mails from churches that they did not want me. Heck, I even got e-mails from churches that I did not even apply to that did not want me. What was wrong with me?

If only I could get a job, anything, all would be well. Everything would be better once I was working full-time again. Come on, God, cooperate, you big stupid jerk. I am sick of this character building!

This time, this terrible free time felt endless. Would anyone ever want me to work again? Would I be a drain and disappointment to my family, an embarrassment? I could see no purpose to the time. I could not see that I was waiting or preparing. What had happened to my belief that everything has a reason? What had happened to my belief that God had a purpose for me?

All of a sudden, people started calling. They asked, "Will I please work for them?" I thought that once I got a position I would immediately feel better, everything would be better, right? Right? In what feels like a moment, my situation is reversed. People want me. I am not being rejected. No one is asking why I am unemployed or what is wrong with me. No one ever really was asking those questions. So why don't I feel magically better? What do I do now with all this anger I was hanging onto that I did not even realize was there before?

I am reminded of the man who cannot walk who Jesus heals with: "Stand up, take your bed and go to your home" (Matthew 9:6). The man wanted healing. His friends wanted his healing. The scribes wanted to debate. Jesus heals the man immediately, but did anyone really expect that the man would be healed? Did the man really expect to be healed?

Like the scribes, I wonder if he too wondered why he could not walk. Was he paralyzed because of his sins? After Jesus heals him, does he wonder why he could not have walked before? At the same time, those questions are now moot. He is healed, and he can walk. He is no longer who he was. Whatever he had planned for that afternoon is definitely changed.

Maybe he was so used to living his life a certain way, thinking that if only he was healed, everything would be perfect. I wonder if he asked God why he was afflicted. What was the purpose? All of a sudden, he can walk. His miracle is for the glory of God, but why?

I asked why. Why did finding a position take all this time? What was the purpose of this time? Was this time for the glory of God? Really? And I felt angry.

At first, I did not want to even realize I was angry. Certainly, I felt anxious about this time. I worried, but I did not think I was angry. Then I realized I was angry, and I did not want to admit I was angry. I felt that I should not have been angry. Somehow I should have understood that all this time was for my benefit and good. Yeah right!

I was angry because I felt hurt. I felt embarrassed because I was not working, and I could not seem to get a new position as a rector. I wondered why I could not find a new position quickly. Why did finding a position take so much time? I felt like I was being punished by God for being stupid.

I should never have talked to my ex-boss. I should never have written a sassy blog with my friend. I should never have worn white shoes after Labor Day.

I was angry that I could not control my feelings and emotions. Why couldn't I just brush off the hurt I felt after leaving my former position? Why couldn't I just turn off the embarrassment I felt? Why couldn't I just control my feelings? Why couldn't I get thrilled and excited about a new position immediately? Because whether I like it or not, I cannot control how I feel. The longer I try to control my feelings, the longer the Spirit will wait until I am ready to feel them.

The Spirit will wait until I am ready to feel. The Spirit will wait until we are ready to feel. Wisdom loudly calls us to her table, to eat and to drink wisdom, but we must come to the table. We must feel what we feel to learn what Wisdom, what the Spirit will teach.

I felt so sure that this time was a waste, a punishment for some unknown crime. I cried that I was a victim, not responsible for my situation. I could not have made any decisions. Then I believed that every decision I made was a foolish decision. Wisdom finally asked: Are you certain that you are correct in all these assumptions?

Was all this time a waste? No, all this time was not a waste. I saw my child walk with my own eyes. I did not hear about her first steps from a daycare worker. I wanted to see my beautiful child as much as possible. Had I not prayed and hoped for her? How many other women did I know received nine months of maternity leave?

Was I a victim? No, I am not a victim. I made decisions. I realized that I did not like my former position, and more important, I realized I did not like where I was as a person. The decision I made to talk to my former boss about my position that day was not the decision that I first made. I made that decision the day I decided to take my daughter home from foster care. I decided to say yes to a faithful life. I would make decisions not out of fear but out of faith.

My leaving my old position was a consequence of the journey to faith and integrity. I could have lied to my boss, and told him that I just loved working for him. I could have said I would never leave, with one eye on the door. No, I told the truth because if I am going to be a truthful person, I need to tell the truth.

Was every decision I made foolish? Nope. My decisions might not have been prudent, but they were made out of faith and integrity. The life of faith is not an easy life. In the past I thought that if one lived a life of integrity that life should be easier, but it is not.

The faithful life is a faithful life. This life is not filled with worldly rewards. You might look like a fool to the outside observer. Your life is not easy, but your life is full. My life is full.

My life is full. My life is full of a hearty laugh that my daughter makes when she is truly delighted. She sounds like a little Frenchman from a cartoon. My life is full of opportunities for joy. I have the time to listen to what the Spirit is saying, and how the Spirit is moving in my life and the life of others.

I wanted to say that all this time has been a terrible burden and misery. I wanted to say that I am a failure for not becoming a rector immediately after leaving my former position. I wanted to say that not making money was stupid (I may still agree with this last statement). With all these statements, I realize that these are about my ego and not about where God might be leading me.

I wondered why it has taken me so many months to understand why I could not just get a new position. Why could I not just figure out why I needed this time? Because I needed this time to learn what I refused to learn when I was working full-time. Because I ignored the hints over and over again about what God was telling me about myself, my faith life, and my ministry to God. I am stubborn and proud. Those two characteristics make for a lousy student. This time has forced me into transformation, and unfortunately, transformation is neither optional nor easy. If I wanted new life, I would need to transform.

In order to have this new life, I need to let the old life die. I need to let my old assumptions, my pride, and ego die. Perhaps all those old wineskins needed to be thrown away or buried, so I could get new wineskins to receive new wine and life again.

So now the faithful journey continues. I am going in a direction I never thought I would before. I am following where the Spirit blows.

16

New Plan: Listen to What God Says

I AM SITTING IN FRONT OF my computer, at my dining room table in a new home, in a new town. My beloved daughter is sleeping in her crib in the other room. Tomorrow we have church.

I look back at these pages, and I am amazed at where I am. This was not what my life was supposed to look like. I had a plan, but I guess that God had a plan as well.

My plan would have avoided every mistake, every foolish decision, and every chance for heartache. My plan would have also avoided love, healing, and growth. I would have preferred to learn those lessons through a correspondence course, but I would not have as many charming stories to tell my daughter when she is older.

Part 2

Life gives us magic

And life brings us tragedy

Everyone suffers some loss

Still we have faith in it,

Childlike hope

There's a reason that outweighs the cost

And gravity throws all these rules in our way

And sometimes the spirit refuses to play

Only the ones who believe

Ever see what they dream

Ever dream what comes true

—"The Color of Roses"
by Beth Nielsen Chapman

17

Pulling at Threads

I PULLED AT THE THREAD.

I thought it was one of those random threads that materializes on your clothing during the course of the day. I was wearing my black funeral skirt. We clergy have those go-to outfits for particular rituals, skirts and jackets and pants that match our clergy shirts. Episcopal priests wear "clericals," these less than flattering clergy shirts—black with what many call the "dog collar." But the collars my dog wears are much more stylish than the white bands of polished cotton or pressed plastic stamped with faux stitching that we clergy wrap around our necks to proclaim our ordained status to the world, because nothing says holy like an ill-fitting shirt and plastic wrapped around our necks.

The fashionista's mantra is that anything goes with black. Perhaps, but not the dreadful, ill-fitting black clergy shirts foisted upon us when we are ordained.

"The Holy Spirit has come upon you and consecrated you to care for God's people. Oh, and just so you don't get too haughty, wear this clergy shirt that will make you look like a shapeless, formless void."

God moved over the shapeless, formless void to begin Creation, so I suppose mirroring them in clericals is not so bad. I wear them when I minister at sacramental occasions like Eucharists, baptisms, weddings, and funerals. I wear them to hospitals and places where I have to visibly be a priest. Clergy shirts are a uniform, basically. I do jazz up the uniform with a fashion sense formed by many years of adoring clothes and shoes in glossy magazines and a fair amount of seeing pictures of myself in college in the 80s, when I had questionable taste in fashion. I have the elegant yet appropriate wedding skirt in a blush pink with a pair of marbleized leather kitten heels and the pastel tweed jacket, in case it's a bit chilly. I have the professional suit not in black, but a precise beige tweed (because only Johnny Cash could carry off black pants and a black blazer and a black shirt). The suit is for the events where the Reverend Laurie Brock is summoned, she who is completely pulled together and will say the appropriate prayer to open the council meeting or will lead the witty and thought-provoking spiritual retreat. And I have the funeral skirt with sensible black heels or flats, depending on if the funeral will involve standing in a muddy graveyard. Heels and muddy earth are not a match made in heaven—a lesson I've learned from experience.

The funeral skirt is well-worn and well-made. A decade of ministry means it's been used many, many times. More times than I care to remember. I've worn it to bury dear parishioners who died suddenly, and those who died after very long illnesses. Neither is easy. I've worn it to be present to those I've known very well and, after I've said the words that priests say to offer some measure of comfort in grief, I've cried in the privacy of my car and shoved a damp handkerchief in its pocket after I wiped away my own tears. Then, for the next funeral, I've discovered the rumpled handkerchief and wondered, for a distant moment, who I'd buried last. The bliss of ignorance gives us those fleeting moments, where we don't remember our grief. Then we do.

I've worn the skirt to bury those children of God who were unknown to me, and my sadness was only in seeing the friends and family of the one who had died feel their grief and remembering my own grief at people who were important and loving in my life. Those funerals always feel uncomfortable to me, yet they are part of ministry. The family of the person who has died calls the church, because a decade ago they visited for Christmas or Easter or came to a wedding or even a funeral there, and since we don't belong to a church, could you do the service? And I do. Early in my ministry, my mentor told me, "People can always go somewhere else for the celebration of a wedding, but not too many places are open to the grief of a funeral."

I know many priests who complain about weddings, but I know many, many more who love to involve themselves in these celebrations, whether or not they know the people getting married. The flowers and tulle and Canon in D invite us into the fantasy of pretty and perfect, at least in that moment.

Funerals are another matter. There are no magazines touting the latest mother of the deceased fashions or the tested and tasty appetizers to serve at the reception. Our modern incarnation of funerals has tried very hard to pretty up grief and loss with nuanced lighting and satin-lined coffins, yet grief remains in its honest and raw state. And my mentor was right. The church, for all its gifts, is a place where people should be able to go in the broken moments, in the moments that aren't swathed in tulle and pretty, but are smothered by dark and empty with no tidy answers to questions our tears ask.

The church, given its confession of death and resurrection, ought to be a community where the mysteries of death, transformation, and eventual resurrection are welcomed, even if their presence pulls at the uncomfortable and even painful threads within us. After almost a decade of ministry, I was about to discover the church, like all things human, could fail at being a community where grief, struggle, and discernment were honored. I was about to discover that even in the Holy Mother Church who worships Jesus, the ultimate troublemaker, those of us who dared to live into the great deep of God would be cast out as trouble-makers too. I was about to learn that the church and her priests could break my heart.

At this funeral, we were burying John, a fellow priest who'd died of cancer. I was sitting in my office, reflecting on how death cuts short expectations. This priest arrived with energy and ideas, and in the short time I'd worked with him, I'd felt re-energized about my ministry with the infusion of his ideas and the implicit permission he'd given to share mine.

And now he was gone.

In my solemn party of one, I noticed a stray thread on my leg and reached to pull it away. It wasn't a stray thread. It was a thread strongly attached to the hem of my trusty funeral skirt. I pulled. And pulled, because one's first response to resistance is usually to pull harder. And watched the hem of my skirt disintegrate.

So here I sat, in my appropriate sadness with my hem undone. I was fine showing my sadness in public. I was not fine showing the raw edge of my skirt. After rummaging through my desk drawer hoping that the Readiness Fairies had put an emergency sewing kit in my desk unbeknownst to me (because I most assur-edly had not put one in my desk), I contemplated my options: the stapler or the roll of tape.

My skirt was well-made, and I wasn't willing to puncture the fabric with staples, so the tape won. I knew it wouldn't hold well, but I also realized it only had to hold until I got vested for the funeral. Centuries ago, church patriarchs and perhaps some matriarchs donned the daily wear of the ordinary Roman citizen to lead services in the church. They were dressed as those they gathered with to pray. Albs and chasubles were *de rigueur*, known then as undergarments and outer cloaks. Time marched on, fash-ions changed, but church fashion did not. So today, to celebrate the Holy Eucharist or lead worship, I wear Roman fashion from the fourth century.

Which, at this moment, meant that whatever my personal

modern clothing looked like underneath, my exterior would show a neatly pressed and perfectly fitted cassock and gleaming white surplice. No one would suspect that earlier that day, I'd haphazardly reached to flick a thread off my stockings, and instead ripped the hem out of the skirt I'd worn for yet another funeral. No one would suspect that in the quiet of my office, I'd pulled at a thread that undid more than the hem of my skirt.

As a daughter of the South, a daughter of good Southern families, my very cells knew how to look pressed and perfect on the outside, no matter what. Realize your husband has been having an affair two days before your sister's wedding? Not a problem. Put on the perfectly fitted dress paired with the heels that are sassy yet practical for dancing all night. Smile and smile again, and save the tears for when you are alone. Stayed up far too late on the day before a big job presentation? Nothing more concealer and the right shade of pink in a shirt can't hide. Realize the life you woke up in is not the one that makes your heart sing? Put on the funeral suit, fix the hem, and go forth into the world.

Perhaps all women struggle with this ability, but as I checked myself in the mirror, I began to cry again because I wasn't all women. I was Laurie, and I wondered why John's death felt so overwhelming, but didn't give myself too much time to wonder. After all, I had to be a priest. The Reverend Laurie Brock had duties and responsibilities that did not include crying or delving into deep emotions at this particular moment. She had expectations to be the charming girl priest at St. Paul's, the parish where I currently served. I had on the uniform. My clergy shirt was pressed. My skirt, even with its temporary hem, looked sharp and elegant. My hair was pulled back appropriately. The few tears I had cried in my office hadn't even done too much damage to my mascara. God bless waterproof mascara.

I wanted to look pulled together, and I did. I didn't want to feel the sadness or grief.

I simply wanted to wear the perfect dress with the perfect heels and live in the perfect home and work in the perfect church. And I did.

But I simply couldn't resist pulling at that damn imperfect thread.

18

Bleeding, Leaving, and Crying

FTER APPLYING A DUAL ANESTHETIC of profanity and Neosporin to my bleeding knee, I sat on the stairs in my empty townhouse in Mobile, Alabama, and cried. I cried because I'd ripped a few layers of skin off my knee when I missed the step at my backdoor while loading my car of yet more personal belongings for my pending move to Louisiana. I cried because I was moving, leaving my faith community and personal community where I'd served for almost five years for a new ministry in an unfamiliar town in an equally unfamiliar state. I cried because I had acute anxiety about closing on my first home in this foreign land where people ate crawfish and gumbo and cheered for the Louisiana State University Tigers and hated the Alabama Crimson Tide. I had been a Crimson Tide fan my entire life. I cried because somewhere in this hurricane of emotions, I knew God was in the center, still and solid as always.

Actually, that annoyed more than comforted me.

I was in the storm of anxiety, grief, and when I allowed it, some fleeting happiness over the something new that I was entering, but I wasn't fully ready for that part yet. I clamored for my inner Jeremiah, the prophet who spent about two-thirds of his prophecy kvetching in a grand way, even accusing God of seducing then raping him with prophecy.

No one could ever accuse Jeremiah of burying his anger.

Right now, with my bleeding knees and aching soul, his words had a place in my mouth. In the world of full-time Christian ministry, we love, and I mean *LOVE*, to talk about where God is calling us. We talk about prayer and discernment as if it's a decision between the lobster and the filet mignon on the dinner menu. Or chocolate and more chocolate. We think God's call is exactly what we want, as if responding to God's call in our lives is akin to submitting the list of classes you'd like to take this semester and getting an orderly schedule back with your earliest class at 10:00 a.m. and no classes on Fridays.

"Whom shall I send to help my people? Who will tell of my great love, with absolutely no inconvenience to your own life?"

Me! Me! I'll go! Send me.

Except that we added the last qualifying line about "no inconvenience." God really just asks the first line.

Going forth means moving, and moving, and going away from comfort and friends. Moving away from prior mindsets and stubborn theology that is narrower than God asks. Moving away from what we want to what God wants.

Years before, when I drove away from the womb of seminary, where I lived in the most amazing city on earth (New York), among the most amazing people I knew (my classmates), and down the street from a Whole Foods and a local coffee shop where they knew my name and my regular order, I cried. Convinced I would never again find a community as wholly joyful and amazing as this one and I would never again shop at a Whole Foods, I gave myself permission to sob uncontrollably to the Pennsylvania border. I cried until I drove into my new home in one of the least amazing towns on earth in lower Alabama (my opinion at the time) where I would begin my ordained life.

I had returned to Mobile fresh out of seminary in New York City. I had lived in Mobile for three years in my preseminary career as an attorney. I left a woman with a law degree who had worked in legal services, handling everything from sexual harassment cases to homeless men trying to get a library card. I arrived three years later a woman ordained in the Holy Mother Church.

I was still profoundly sad and convinced I would never be happy in Alabama, but little by little, I discovered new friends and rediscovered old ones. I found a favorite Vietnamese restaurant and a woman who taught me voice lessons when I decided I wanted to learn how to sing. I worked with Albert, who was the rector at Holy Name Church, and he had been a priest in the church longer than I had been alive when I was ordained. Our working relationship was a surprising joy. He was at the end of his official paid ministry; I, at the beginning. My liberal viewpoints and his traditional conservative sense found respect and admiration in each other. We loved Anglican chant and disagreed on how often Elizabethan language should be used in church services. We had also suffered together, as we both were wounded by some parishioners who reacted with lashing words and actions after the consecration of the first openly gay bishop in the Episcopal Church. With Albert, I felt heard because I was heard. So when the rector of my first parish in Mobile, Alabama, told me he was retiring, I realized my life as a priest would mean leaving a place I loved. Again.

As I considered my next call, I thought about the expectation of the church—that I go to a bigger parish, that I make more money, and that I add a more impressive title to my resumé. Moving up the corporate ladder is as much of the fabric of the church as it is in the business world. I also wanted to be safe. I spent the last couple of years in my first parish feeling like the unsafe victim of some of my parishioners, who vented the rage they felt about the church's openness to gay people on their clergy. A few members of the parish vestry, the governing committee of a local Episcopal church, questioned my own sexual identity, because apparently if one is a single woman of a certain age, one must be a closeted lesbian. A few vestry members wanted me to sign a declaration that I believed homosexuality to be contrary to God's law; others wanted me to submit my sermons to them before I preached them for review and editing. I did neither. I was, however, profoundly hurt by their actions.

All of this had gone with me to the interview in Louisiana. The rector, a tall, burly man who looked as if he could have moonlighted as a bouncer in a sketchy bar, picked me up at the hotel and took me to a restaurant where I would meet the other clergy on staff. He wanted us all to have dinner to see if we "played well together." On the drive there, he talked at length about how he wore cowboy hats and promised the search committee of St. Paul's that he would never use incense during worship. He listed the impressive statistics of St. Paul's, their million-dollar budget (larger than the diocese, he noted), the large number of members (largest in the diocese, he noted), the first-rate school (the best in the diocese, he noted), and the retired bishops in residence (several rectors of St. Paul's have been elected bishop, he noted). On paper, St. Paul's was a successful parish.

Later in his office, I told him about my experience at Holy Name, of feeling unprotected from the anger of certain parishioners. He stretched out behind his desk that was as large as the conference table at Holy Name and replied that he always protected his clergy, because that was his job. When I told him how much I had been hurt by their words and actions, he assured me he would never let that happen to one of his priests and he would always have the backs of those who worked under him. "We aren't just colleagues here, we're friends," I recalled from my official visit.

He showed me again the large budget of the parish, and told me I had been underpaid at my current parish. He would give me a substantial pay raise and a job title that reflected my increased clergy responsibility, although he offered no official job description. He also told me I would be the first female priest at the parish, and went on to tell me how he'd approached this with the vestry by saying that if they wanted another male priest, they could have one, but they wouldn't be getting the best candidate.

My ego felt quite good. A pay raise, a great title of "associate rector," and a large parish. This would look great on my resumé. Bigger is better, even in the church, right?

This was the focus of my visit. I hadn't inquired much about the spiritual space and life of the church. Yes, I'd seen a Sunday Eucharist, slipping in unnoticed by most to observe the fundamentals of a service. I'd toured the huge complex, and I'd met the staff and some parishioners, who were all lovely people. Nothing deeper was offered to me, and I didn't ask. I just nodded.

I couldn't sleep that night in the hotel. I kept asking in my prayers if this was the place I was called. I sat in the middle of the king-sized hotel bed with four thousand pillows and felt incompetent.

So, in the wee hours of the morning, I called my friend Brad. He'd recently accepted a call as rector to another parish, so he had some experience of discerning a new job. And he wouldn't hate me for waking him up.

Or he'd get over being mad at me for waking him up.

"So how was the visit?" he asked, still half-asleep.

I told him all about the pay raise and the official title. "And he said he protected his clergy."

"That probably made you feel good."

"I'm tired of feeling unsafe in the church," I replied.

Not feeling safe is one of my great wounds. As a child, growing up with parents who did not get along particularly well and who allowed their frustration with their marriage to spill out in anger, I rarely felt safe, except under the bed. When they would begin to fight, I would slip around my bed to the side closest to the wall and burrow under it. My safe space had an ample supply of stuffed animals to keep me company. I cried at school when I was in third grade after I realized I would keep growing and one day, I would be too big to fit under the bed. Where, then, could I go when I felt unsafe?

The church seemed like a good option, this community of people who proclaimed love and acceptance. I wasn't completely naive; I realized the church was capable of being hurtful and petty. Humans, after all, comprised its ranks. I just didn't know emotional crucifixion was still on the menu until my experience at Holy Name. But surely, I thought, that was an anomaly, limited to a particular set of circumstances involving the consecration of an openly gay man as a bishop and some very rage-filled people.

Brad didn't say anything. I heard him yawn, then apologize.

"How do I know if this is where I'm called to be?" I asked, starting to cry.

"Who the hell knows," he offered. "But maybe wherever we end up is where God is calling us for one reason or another."

I hate when Brad speaks that kind of truth that doesn't offer a tidy solution, but instead invites risk. What was "call" after all? We in the business of full-time Christian service love to use words like "discernment" and "vocation" and "call" to speak of the irrational and unexplainable mystery of trotting after God in our lives. Mystery is a feeling that simply is. Much like the Supreme Court's definition of pornography, mystery isn't explainable, but I know it when I experience it.

Some people may be born with the ability to sit in the deep mystery of God's siren song and listen. Maybe all are born with that part of our soul firmly in tact. But many of us let it slip away as the more "mature" qualities of logic and intellectual rationalization take up a greater part of our decision making. I didn't want God's siren song. I wanted the one that made all my fears go away. I wanted to walk away and start new.

What I know now is that we can't explain these, or at least I can't, because the deepest surge in my soul as I follow the trail of love and fear is not rationalized or verbalized. It is simply felt and, after a time of terror and desire, desire wins by the slimmest margin.

Of course, in my blissful ignorance, I let fear have the slim margin and simply made a list overflowing with rationality. I was moving up the ecclesiastical ladder. The other priests seemed like nice guys. And I would be safe because the boss said I would. So in my mind, I was called.

The rector offered me the job before I left. I felt hesitant, but remembered the logical list. He told me he would give me a week to think about accepting the position. He gave me four days before he called to ask me again, although it was more like a reminder that this was my new place. I formally accepted the invitation to serve as the associate rector for youth and young adults.

I visited my new city later and bought my very first home—a condominium in a complex that had been renovated. The kitchen had brand-new stainless steel appliances, and the bathrooms had beautiful granite. There was a fireplace and lovely hardwood. And it had a screened-in back porch that ran the length of the condo. The porch sold me.

Now, as I cried with my skinned knee, I felt very, very unsafe. But I put the last of my plants in the car, leaving two geraniums with my neighbor Sally. I stood in the doorway of my home in Mobile and prayed.

"Thank you for being my home."

I shut the door and limped to my car to drive to this new place where I hoped God was calling me. And I gave myself permission to cry to the Louisiana state line.

19

Fine, Except I Hurt

I LIKED MY NEW JOB AS sassy girl priest, the kid sister of this kingdom of priests, as Robert, one of the fellow priests on staff called us when we posed for a group picture, all wearing matching stoles, or, as the rector called them, our "gang colors." There were four in the gang of clergy at St. Paul's. I began to meet new parishioners. I preached sermons and celebrated the Eucharist and became one of the friends that all the priests at St. Paul's were supposed to be to each other. We had school chapel and coffee and lunch together. At the end of all the associates' reports at vestry, we all said, "And I love my job."

Robert had brought me into the work of planning the service for the archbishop of Canterbury's visit to New Orleans, which tapped into my love of all things spiritual and liturgical. I sat with Robert on the stage with the archbishop of Canterbury and the presiding bishop of the Episcopal Church in the United States and felt quite happy. I thought, "If they could see me now." I explored my new city and state, finding good restaurants and quirky clothing stores. I discovered Baton Rouge had far too much concrete for my taste, but where I lived was a little natural haven.

I really loved the space of my new home. I started spending

time on my back porch, which I named "The Chapel." My neighborhood, flush with trees, had beautiful hawks that were active in the morning when I drank my coffee and in the evening as I cooled down from my run. I sat on my back porch, sweated from the miles of roadwork, prayed my evening prayers, and watched the hawks soar.

During my first fall in St. Paul's, I went to the clergy conference, a gathering of Episcopal priests from a diocese, a geographical area, sort of like states in the Episcopal Church. I met another newly arrived priest in the diocese, Mary Koppel. She'd just arrived at St. Christopher's in New Orleans from Hawaii. Robert introduced us and said, "When I wanted you to come to Louisiana, I thought you would be the new Mary, but now that you're both here, this could be trouble."

In our first encounter, we both smiled at each other and said pleasant hellos. My rector soon corralled the St. Paul's clergy into our gang, as he liked to call us, to leave the conference to go somewhere else. Later that evening, Mary and I ended up walking to our rooms together and talking.

I asked her about Hawaii. She asked me about Alabama. We heard each other's stories about our paths to ordination and why we were where we were now. Mary had come home to New Orleans, where her family had lived for generations. I had ventured into a completely new place. As we walked, a couple of the older clergy in the diocese asked if we were sisters. Apparently, we even looked alike.

And we both discovered we had quite the taste for Cracker Barrel. Lucky for us, there was a Cracker Barrel conveniently located about halfway between New Orleans and Baton Rouge, so we decided to begin meeting there for lunch once a month. Over monthly orders of chicken and dumplings (me) and meatloaf (Mary), we talked about how terrible clergy shirts looked on women with any good-size boobs; how her marriage was feeling unsteady; how my current boyfriend seemed nice enough, but I wondered; and how working under our current bosses was some-times fun and sometimes difficult.

We talked about our jobs. Both of us worked with youth and young adults in our respective churches. We talked about some upcoming outreach projects we could do together. We talked about school chapel services and how much we liked time we spent with children's ministry. We both engaged in the litany of what we liked about our positions and the parishioners with whom we spent time. I was discovering I really found great joy in the services I led at the local retirement homes. Children and elderly people have a brash honesty as they share stories and ask questions that is both comforting and challenging.

After I mixed my mashed potatoes and gravy into a well-blended fusion of deliciousness, I finally asked Mary, "Do you ever feel like window-dressing instead of a priest?" We were both just past our one-year anniversaries at our respective parishes.

Mary nodded. "Kind of like you get the jobs they don't want to do, and they make a big deal about having you on staff because you have these." Mary pointed to her breasts.

"Kind of like my job is to be the sassy kid sister and not the priest," I added. "But it's fine," I added, as a salve to the true feeling.

I felt fine in my job, my second paid job as a priest. Not great, not unhappy, but fine, that neutral, numbing place of okay that is sustainable enough to make you stay put and not ask too many questions. I had friends and a home and a job. I worked with priests and went out for drinks with them after a long day. That was all fine. A clergy colleague says "fine" is an acronym for freaked out, insecure, neurotic, and emotional.

I don't think fine has that much energy. Fine is the five pounds you know you could lose so all your clothes would fit better, but losing the lard would take some level of work you just aren't willing to do, so you stick with the elastic waistbands. Fine is just, well, fine. It was safe and predictable.

The waitress came and asked if we wanted dessert, which is

never a real question for either Mary or me. Of course we do. After we'd devoured blackberry cobbler with ice cream, we stood up to leave, and Mary noticed me wince.

"My hip is hurting," I explained. It had been hurting for the past few months. At first, it was just a twinge, but over the last six months, there were days where walking was a serious effort.

"That's what you get for exercising and staying fit." She laughed, then gave me that listen-to-me-I'm-not-kidding look that would make her a great mother one day. "But seriously, go get it checked out. That doesn't seem fine."

I'm no fan of going to the doctor, for many reasons. One negative side effect of being a priest is our frequent interaction with tragic illnesses. We hear the stories of the aching back that was pancreatic cancer or the headache that was an inoperable brain tumor. And we know the names of people we've loved and watch die who go with those stories.

I also had the best doctor ever in seminary, who was a master of the mind-body-spirit connection. Whenever I would get a cold that I couldn't shake, that took root in my lungs and produced that disgusting hacking cough that drew dirty looks from fellow seminarians during the worship silences and made me wonder if I had typhoid, he would ask me to bring my calendar into his office. The schedule I was keeping was as important to him as the virus in my system. His prescriptions were often for a day or two in my pajamas in my home and no contact with anyone except Jane Austen. Costume dramas have done more to heal my exhausted self than many antibiotics.

My spirit and mind might be very good at intellectualizing my way out of exhaustion, sadness, unrest, or whatever ill-timed emotion I'm avoiding; my physical self is a loud, attention-getting broad. She will not be ignored, and the other two of them use the third as a messenger because often I'm not paying attention to what my soul is saying.

But I dismissed my hip pain as life edging into middle age.

I went to a massage therapist instead. She asked me where she should focus her magic hands, I rattled off the usual—shoulders, back, then added, "Oh, and my hip hurts."

I had a long, logical discourse on why my hip hurt. I run. I hadn't been stretching properly. I was getting older. I was running longer distances on concrete sidewalks. The massage therapist nodded and said, "The hips are where women move forward. I wonder what's holding you back."

I do not generally hear these Yoda-esque statements as a voice from God. I hear them as people who are interfering in my life. Except that's exactly what God does—interferes in our lives. A statement of physiology and an "I wonder" comment were far from the certainty I wanted. I wanted an hour-long massage that would make me feel better and let me continue on my desired journey. I wanted to continue with fine. I did not want someone to ask a question I myself wasn't even willing to ask. And I certainly did not want that from a person who was supposed to infuse me with relaxation and self-care for the next hour.

While I knew intellectually my hip was likely a pulled muscle, all sorts of possible horrible illnesses and situations, not helped by my searches on Web MD, kept me away from the doctor's office. Mary, however, played the friend-mother to me enough over the next few weeks until I finally went. At some point in my recent life, the physical therapist diagnosed, I had torn a muscle in my hip. Regular physical therapy over months would help strengthen it. My physical therapist told me it would be hard work to repair a muscle that had been torn and left to heal improperly. Phrases like "scar tissue" and "worse before it feels better" reverberated in my mind on the drive home from his office.

I kept wondering how I could tear a hip muscle and not notice that kind of wound. And why was it hurting so much now? And why did the question from the massage therapist bother me so much? Hips were just, well, joints in my body with big muscles wrapped around them, muscles I apparently can tear and not notice. I had an injury, plain and simple.

An injury that would get better with therapy and work. I took an Advil before going to bed that night, because my hip had started to hurt mostly around the clock by now.

I tried to sleep.

My painful hip, however, was swigging a glass of bourbon and looking at my soul, saying, "It's going to be a bumpy night."

And oh, was she ever right.

20

Filled with Heaviness

I touched John's body for the last time. Like all people who have died and been prepared by morticians, he felt cold and hard, like the space previously filled by his soul had been filled by concrete. When I laid my hands on him to pray during my final visit to the hospital before he died, his skin was cool and soft. His arm moved under the touch of my hand, and I felt him breathe. I also felt him slipping through the thin place.

Ancient people understood thin places as the space between the boundaries of our world and the other worlds that become, well, thin. The popularity of Celtic Christianity brought the term full-force into Christian spiritual vocabulary, mostly to my annoyance. I've heard people use thin places when describing some particularly warm and cuddly spiritual moment. And use it. And use it. Thin places seem to be nice lovely spaces where heaven and earth meet, Disney music swells, birds sing, and all is right with the world. Perhaps for some.

The thin places I have experienced are more akin to the precious space that separates the raging hurricane from the calm eye. They are at once preternaturally peaceful and as terrifying as standing on a crumbling ledge thousands of feet above the earth.

I almost always experience them when a soul is passing from this realm to heaven. When the thin place passes over, heaviness remains.

"You all sit over there and say psalms," I heard a priest say to me and another priest present. I felt the heaviness of John's body once more before I lifted my hand to do as I was told. We began to read.

> *As the deer longs for the water-brooks,*
>
> *so longs my soul for you, O God.*
>
> *My soul is athirst for God, athirst for the living God;*
>
> *when shall I come to appear before the presence of God?*
>
> (Psalm 42, BCP)

Three men gathered around John's body to dress him in his alb, a stole, and a chasuble, all part of the clothing many clergy wear when celebrating the Eucharist. Vesting a priest in the clothing of his or her office is an ancient tradition, one that I was newly experiencing on this day. As the men gathered in the room to take direction from one of the priests who had done this many times, the mortician started cutting things across the back to get the clothing on the body. For the first time I saw that underneath all of the clothes on anyone who has died and will be laid in state, there is a plastic suit. Nothing natural, just plastic, next to our skin. I asked the mortician later why, and he explained that it keeps the embalming fluid from leaking out. I decided in that moment cremation or a totally natural burial are the best options for me.

I wondered why what we wear after we die matters. I wondered if John had wanted to be vested, or if this was the idea of the clergy who were vesting him. Don't we come before the presence of the living God in our most authentic selves? And yet, we continue to cover ourselves with vestments of our lives, even in death. A favorite dress or a uniform. Makeup. Yes, all who lay in state wear a heavy amount of makeup. And we are still dead.

My tears have been my food day and night,

while all day long they say to me, "Where now is your God?"

I pour out my soul when I think on these things:

how I went with the multitude and led them into the house of God,

With the voice of praise and thanksgiving,

among those who keep holy-day.

The last Eucharist John celebrated was Christmas Day. The next Sunday he was in church to celebrate the Eucharist, but he'd been so sick he couldn't sit up. I told him to go home. He and I talked about how winter colds were the worst, because that's what was wrong with him. Just a cold.

John had arrived at St. Paul's a few months before, after Robert had accepted a position in a church in Texas. I missed Robert, but found John to be filled with energy and ideas and a deep spirituality. In our talks together, I heard a hope for a renewal of my ministry—dreams for what God may be calling me to do as a priest. I told him I sometimes thought I was here to play a role dictated by the rector, and he suggested I rewrite the script. Whenever I would start to say something outrageous, like leading a church group to walk to Santiago de Compostela in Spain, I would stop before I finished stating the dream aloud. John would look at me, smile, and say, "Keep talking."

And I would. We would sit in his office for hours discussing the wonder of life and the wonder of being called to ministry. I told him he was the priest I wanted to be when I grew up. He told me never to grow up.

Then he got a cold that never went away, and the cold wasn't a cold; it was cancer. And then he began to go away. While John took his last, grand journey, the parish life went along, short one priest. While we tried to love our friend and colleague to the last seconds of his life here, the parish life went along. And while we stood at his funeral, life went on.

Why are you so full of heaviness, O my soul?

and why are you so disquieted within me?

Put your trust in God;

for I will yet give thanks to him, who is the help of my counte-
nance, and my God.[2]

I was full of heaviness, and I wondered out loud at a morning coffee with the other priests on staff, now only three of us, if we might need to talk to someone about our grief. I was summarily told, "No."

Then I wondered why my then-bishop had asked Mary if I felt bullied at St. Paul's. He had approached her after John's funeral to speak with her. As I was taking off my vestments in my office and checking to see if the hem of my skirt was still behaving, she repeated the conversation.

"He told me that my friend needed to be loved a bit more today, then asked me if I thought you were being bullied here or if you felt bullied."

I stopped taking off my vestments. "Why would he say that? That's an odd question, one he shouldn't be asking you," I said, hearing my voice tense.

"I'm just repeating what he said," Mary offered, defending against my rising anger.

"I know. You know the bishop and the rector don't get along. It just feels like . . . " I stopped, not really knowing what it felt like. And hearing the word "bullied" bothered me. I was a strong woman, certainly not the kind of person who could be bullied. And the rector was my friend. Friends don't bully friends.

We walked down the hall and out of the church office building. We decided to take a break from Cracker Barrel on this day, so the monumental task of where we would eat lay before us. I discovered

---

2 Psalm 42 in the *Book of Common Prayer* (New York: Church Publishing, 1979), p. 643.

I am ravenous after funerals, and the appetizers we had eaten earlier were wearing thin.

"Are you concerned?" I asked Mary. She shrugged her shoulders and said I'd been saying I was tired lately, which is almost always my code for "something isn't right, but I don't know what." She suggested I ask the bishop, and I told her I'd think about it. I did, for a few weeks, but then my grandmother began her journey to death, and the bishop's observation fell away.

I wondered about my grandmother, who had fallen and broken her hip the same month John had been diagnosed with cancer. I had been a priest long enough to know how her journey would end, and I felt weary of death.

And I wondered why my soul felt so heavy that it almost felt like nothing at all.

21

Grandmother

I N THE MIDST OF THE illness and death of John, my paternal grandmother fell and broke her hip. She was eighty-nine, and I knew that this was likely an injury from which she wouldn't recover. She lived in Tuscaloosa, several hours away from where I lived. I've always had a sense of frustration at best and anger at worst that I've visited parishioners and family and friends of parishioners in their illnesses and walked with them as far as we humans on this side of the kingdom can go on the holy journey of death, but my vocation often prevents that same privilege for my own family. My grandmother was dying, and my responsibilities at the parish did not allow me to be at her side as I would have liked to be.

Not that I could have done much, and many other members of my family were at her side. I made several trips, but when you realize every visit is likely the last, thousands of quick trips to her bedside would never be enough. As I made my last visit to Tuscaloosa before she died, I sat in her room and told her of my last trip to England. She was absolutely the best audience for those facts you learn on trips that no one else wants to hear.

She loved to travel, and before her health had prevented her jet-setting, she saw the Egyptian pyramids, the Roman Coliseum, and Buckingham Palace. Medication and age had tempered her remarkable mind, so she didn't say much. I told her of the portrait of the Brontë sisters and the sounds of the choir at Westminster Abbey and the particular taste of tea in British tea shops. I showed her pictures of the amazing food I ate and omitted my tour of Scotch distilleries. Granny was a devout Baptist; for decades, we'd concealed the fact that all of her children and grandchildren drank, and I wasn't letting that cat out the bag on her deathbed.

They were stories she'd heard before, but I showed her pictures of the stained glass windows of St. Paul's in London still left unrepaired from the bombs of World War II. She told me in halting words of her life during that era. I told her how cold the Pacific Ocean was, but I waded in it anyway on a recent trip to the Pacific Northwest, so I could say I had walked in the water of both oceans. She shared about her childhood trip to California with an aunt who could only drive a car in forward.

We sat in silence for a long time. I reminded myself I could cry in the room, because this was my grandmother and I didn't need to be a pastoral presence for anyone. So I did. I finally prayed the Lord's Prayer, and she joined me. I told her I loved her, kissed her again, and walked out for what we both knew would be the final time we would see each other on this side of the kingdom.

As a devout Baptist, she had also been rather skeptical of my ordination and ministry in the church. Women were servants in the church, not ordained ministers. When I went to New York to seminary, she had been guardedly supportive—which was more than I could say for my sister and father, who were absolutely sure I had lost my mind. My sister explained to me that I was prone to whims, and my father said he simply didn't understand any of what I was doing. My mother was cautiously optimistic, I suspect partially because my father was so unsupportive. Their divorce a decade ago still had ragged edges. My closest friends reminded me that the most important voice to listen to besides God was the quiet one within my soul. So I listened.

I went to seminary, and when I was ordained to the priesthood, my family sat in the pews. My grandmother received communion from my hands, although I warned her that the Blood of Christ was real wine. I'm still quite sure that was the only time alcohol ever touched her lips. Through the years, we had many conversations about God. After 9/11, she wanted to know more about Islam. We talked about why certain faiths understood and practiced the ordination of women. After she attended a funeral of a friend who was Episcopalian, she remarked that the service didn't say much about her friend. I explained that in the Episcopal Church, a funeral is a remembrance of our baptisms, which are fulfilled in our deaths. I added that everyone from a homeless man to the Queen was buried with the same words.

"That's a nice idea," she remarked.

She even asked about transubstantiation, after she moved into her assisted living residence and started going to all the Christian services they held with her group of friends. I explained the Roman doctrine of how the bread and wine became the body and blood.

"Does the Episcopal Church believe that?"

"No," I replied, still wondering how transubstantiation had come up in conversation at the retirement village. "We pretty much believe that what happens is a holy mystery."

I never knew, however, exactly how she really felt about women being ordained to the priesthood. So when my father called one evening to tell me that Granny has specified that her Baptist pastor would lead the church funeral, and I was to officiate the graveside services, I was surprised. And then not. She would have the church service of her Baptist faith, and she would be committed to God in the voice of her granddaughter.

So after the Baptist preacher talked about Dixie and her life and love of the church, we gathered at the grave. I prayed the words that I have prayed for so many others, but these words were

different. They were my words of grief and hope. My voice was
certain and sure as I prayed, filled with that stillness that is one
of the best gifts God gives at certain crises moments. I tossed the
dirt on her coffin and pronounced the Easter blessing, to which
my youngest nephew offered a loud and hearty, "Amen."

I stood and looked at her coffin. I touched its smoothness and
warmth. The wood had absorbed the May sunlight. I realized
when I started to step to put my prayer book down that my legs
would not move. They were shaking. The clothing of my priesthood hid their fragility, and the parts of me that were public were
quite collected. I myself was the line between the fierceness of a
hurricane and the stillness of the eye. Even at the grave, we make
our song, Alleluia, Alleluia, Alleluia.

And the words of my faith, the rich prayers that accompanied
the poor, the outcast, soldiers, presidents, and royalty to resurrected life, also welcomed Granny to their number.

She probably responded with a question about
transubstantiation.

22

Lost

MARY AND I WERE LOST again.

Neither one of us is particularly adept at getting from one point to another in a succinct and direct way. We have seen back roads and the middle of nowhere regularly on our journeys. Maps aren't useful to either of us, as we obviously failed the map-reading class of life. We wander.

And get lost.

So on this hot, steamy summer day, we were lost along the small towns that dot the Mississippi River in southern Louisiana. Both of us had been asked to help with the Lutheran Church's national youth event. In July, thousands of youth and adults came together in New Orleans to celebrate their faith through prayer and action. A Lutheran pastor friend asked us to help, and we were both thrilled.

We were asked to coordinate a literacy effort in one of the tiny, forgotten towns where most families don't have any books in the home. A local school would serve as the gathering place. So through the months, those coming to New Orleans had gathered thousands of children's books that were free to anyone who came that day. I had planned crafts and games the youth could play with the children who came to visit. We'd been sent directions by the principal. I'd called her back to get more detailed directions that included lots of, "If you see the beached shrimp boat, you've gone too far, so turn around."

I need those markers that remind me when I've gotten really lost and need to turn around.

I laughed as the principal included references in her verbal map to the house Mrs. Herveaux lived in before her husband's death. My grandmother gave directions like that, these short missives on the people and lives they lived along the route you were traveling.

"While you're driving up the road to Fayette from Tuscaloosa, you'll see the white frame house on your left a bit off the road. Mrs. Williams lived there. You remember her. She married the former wide receiver who played for Alabama, and he was a Methodist minister. Do you know him?"

My grandmother, like much of the world, believed that we ministers knew every other minister in the world, or at least the ones in Alabama. Hearing another person give directions like my grandmother made me smile for a fleeting moment, then I remembered I wouldn't hear her give directions like that again.

Armed with detailed directions, Mary and I started on our journey, until her then-husband decided he would tell us a better way to go. So, for an unknown reason, we trusted his directions more and followed his map until we decided we were lost. Very lost. So after some stops at three gas stations and one bait shop, we pieced together our route and arrived late.

Youth and adults were waiting, and we began with prayer and welcomed adults and children to our day of fun with reading. We read books to children, created puppets to act out the stories we read, and played games. For hours, I felt fully engaged in ministry. That I had this feeling as I was working on my own time with another denomination did not escape me. That I had also received a phone call from my mother at 5:00 a.m. to tell me that my stepfather's mother had unexpectedly died also did not escape me, although I simply decided that I did not have the energy to focus on yet one more death right now. I had books to share with children.

A young girl wearing a hot pink shirt decorated with whales and lime-green striped pants and no shoes came into the room with her mother. I greeting them both, and I asked the girl if she liked to read. She nodded. I told her she could pick out some books of her very own. I looked at the tables spilling over with books and said, "Would you like to find some books?"

She nodded.

"What kind of story do you like?"

She pointed to her shirt.

"Whales?"

She nodded. So we went from table to table, looking for a book about whales. After many, many piles of books, I started to offer second options. Wouldn't a book about a tiger be great? She shook her head, "No." She also rejected my offer of the entire Lemony Snickett series. Unicorns were also below par. She was holding out for exactly what she wanted—a book about whales.

Finally, on the end of one table, I spied a whale on a cover. Thanking Jesus, I pulled it out from the stack to discover a book about Jonah and the whale. Jonah is one of my favorite stories in the Bible, and one of my least favorite parts about the Jonah story is the continued mistake that Jonah was swallowed by a whale.

He was not. He was swallowed by a big fish. Not that that slight detail matters much, and my new friend was quite delighted by my find. We sat down at a table to read her book. I asked if she would like to read.

She shook her head. I realized I had spent over twenty minutes in her company, and I had yet to hear her speak. I started to read.

"Jonah was a prophet of God."

"What's a prophet?" Her voice was strong and sure. Not what I expected.

"Someone who tells people what they don't always want to hear." She watched me with her brown eyes, then nodded.

"God wanted Jonah to go to Nineveh," I explained after reading the first few pages where God comes to Jonah with quite a clear directive and Jonah summarily ignores God.

"Where's Nineveh?"

"Far away."

"Where whales live?"

"Near where whales live," I said, not having a clue exactly where Nineveh actually was.

And I continued reading. She looked for several minutes at the page illustrating Jonah's unfortunate encounter with the whale.

"Why did the whale eat Jonah?"

"Because God wanted Jonah to go somewhere and Jonah didn't want to go, so God sent the whale to swallow him and take him to Nineveh."

"Oh. He should have just gone, but then the story wouldn't have a whale. I guess the whale made sure Jonah wouldn't get lost."

I looked down at her. Brown curls fell across her face. She smiled up at me. Thousands of years of theologians extolling the virtues of Jonah, and she sums up the book in a couple of sentences. Where were you in my Old Testament class? I thought.

He should have just gone, but then the story wouldn't have a whale. Or a big fish, which seems to be the most memorable part of the story. After all, who hears the name Jonah and doesn't automatically think of some large sea creature swallowing him? And the whale made sure Jonah wouldn't get lost. When God wants us to go somewhere, God will make sure we get there, even if the way involves being swallowed whole.

We finished the story, she jumped up, excited to take her book home. Her mother came to take her hand. She took a few steps away, then turned around, ran back, and gave me a hug. I hugged her back, then felt the pricks of tears in my eyes. As she ran back to her mother, I walked quickly out the backdoor and began to cry.

In that moment, if someone had come outside and asked me what was wrong, I would have told them that my stepgrandmother had died. Death is always a good excuse to cry, and people almost always say they are sorry and hold your hand or make some other gentle physical reminder that you aren't alone in your grief.

But I knew that the tears formed when the girl talked about Jonah and the whale. The whale made sure Jonah wouldn't get lost, even though being swallowed whole feels like being lost. If someone had come outside and asked me why I was crying, and I told them that line, I'm quite sure I would have gotten the look that says, "Well, I have no idea what to say to that."

Neither did I.

I reminded myself that I had lost three people who were important to me in a short amount of time. I reminded myself that I had close, wonderful friends who loved me. I reminded myself that there were many things about my ministry that gave me life, including what I was doing today.

So why did the story of Jonah and Nineveh feel like a hand-written note from God, delivered via a fashion-forward girl in bare feet?

Why did I even care? I smeared away the last of my tears and decided I was simply tired. I needed some vacation, and I would feel better.

God was not calling me to Nineveh or anywhere else. I was quite fine exactly where I was. All was simply smashing and great. I was exactly where I needed to be, and life was fine here. I loved my job. I was fine.

Lather. Rinse. Repeat.

God, of course, is persistent. Eons of dealing with us humans with our willfulness and stubbornness and sheer stupidity brings out that quality. But God, being God, has several options to get our attention. We ignore the burning bush; God sends a crazy man eating locusts and honey. We think that's blasé; God offers God Incarnate. That seems too ordinary? Well, just wait until the walking on water and resurrection from the dead.

I wasn't listening to that deeply honest inner voice that speaks loudest through tears, so God tried door number two . . . or door number twenty or two hundred. I felt lost. So I began having trouble sleeping. And losing weight, and feeling more and more like I was unsettled, but couldn't figure out for the world why.

Apparently, I was going to Nineveh, one way or the other, for a reason I did not know. I was on a journey to a place I did not want to go. And when I got lost, God let me be swallowed whole.

23

Amid the
Encircling Gloom

I DIDN'T GO TO NINEVEH, BUT I did go to Spain. My grand-mother left all the grandchildren some money, and I wanted to do something with my inheritance that would honor her. Two weeks in a place where I didn't speak the language seemed to fit the bill.

I also wanted to get away from the unrest I felt in my soul. The start of the fall was fast and furious, as expected in a large parish attached to a school. Meetings to attend, schedules to plan, and worship services to pray. With five services on Sunday and two school chapel services during the week, along with a midweek Holy Eucharist, St. Paul's looked like a place of busy spirituality. For me, I felt more like I was punching the time clock for corporate prayer. The liturgical planning at St Paul's from my perspective seemed to occur three minutes before the service began at the front doors of the church when the rector told us who would be praying the opening prayers, who would be leading the creed, and who would be preparing the altar. Mary and I talked frequently about how we missed the prayerful and careful creation of liturgy in which we had participated in our former parishes. In our current positions, the liturgy happened without our thoughts or ideas. Show up, preach, pray, and then go out for coffee or drinks afterwards.

Every church is different, and this seemed to work for the parish, I reasoned. My reason didn't salve the yearning I had for those quiet moments where, in the presence of silence and God, I reflected on the liturgy and drew together scripture, prayers, hymns, music, and silence to create sacred space and time. Maybe the new job responsibilities the rector gave me would fill some of that yearning. Perhaps sensing my unrest, he rearranged my job responsibilities. He hired someone to work with youth and young adults, told me I would be her supervisor, and gave me John's old position, which had been working with spirituality and adult Christian formation. I was initially excited about the change, but the excitement was tempered by unrest in my personal soul that seemed unaffected by my new job description.

I did find joy in time with parishioners, who were good and kind people. I loved the time I spent at local nursing homes and the people I visited there. I found energy with various interfaith and ecumenical projects, particularly the work around HIV/AIDS awareness in Louisiana. The youth confirmation class, a series of classes for those learning more about the Episcopal Church that I'd taught for the past two years, had been life-giving in so many ways. The insights of the faith of the youth, the liturgy we created together, and simply getting to know these incredible young people over the months grounded me in the community we created, and I looked forward to our weekly gatherings. I found surprising comfort and self-expression in the blog Mary and I created and wrote. While hearing criticism from fellow priests for the name "Dirty Sexy Ministry" and what we wrote, we regularly received e-mails from people who were touched and inspired by our essays. In these areas, which were mostly done alone or with other ministers from outside the parish system, I felt sparks of life. This was contrasted with my sense that, piece by piece, I was losing more of my soul than I was fueling with authentic ministry in the system that was my day-to-day job.

I wondered if I was having a crisis of faith. The rector implied that I was. My love of God was fine. My love of the institution and the authority figures in it was anything but. I felt that my self and soul had become co-opted by the expectations and desires of others. I wanted to talk about the loss and grief I had experienced; my understanding was that I was expected to take some vacation time and return to be "fine," or, as so stated by the rector, "the old Laurie." I hoped to be involved in a broad way in the faith community in Louisiana; I heard the rector refer, jokingly perhaps, to the parish as the diocese of St. Paul's, certainly not an indication that we were fans of cooperative ministry. I yearned for conversations with coworkers about spirituality and courageous, insane faith; I heard only silence in this space after John's voice died. I hoped that I would have a life in the parish and a personal life that were separated by an honoring of boundaries; I felt expectations to have no boundaries between the two.

I hoped more of my dreams for ministry, those things that God calls us to do with courage, love, and vision, would matter; I felt expectations to fit into a role that had little to do with my deepest self and sense of ministry, but more about being the sassy kid sister priest in our gang of clergy. I yearned to be heard in my clergy community when I voiced my concerns and doubts instead of hearing why my opinions or thoughts were misinformed. I wanted not to laugh at hurtful and offensive comments passed off as jokes by the clergy, but to say, "Stop, those aren't funny to me," and be heard. I wanted to be able to disagree without having my views heard as threatening or disloyal. What I experienced when I slipped my toe into the waters of honesty was a growl that I clearly understood as, "Do not even think about suggesting there is anything that could be different. If you do, you'll be sorry."

I was right.

During this time, the bishop of the diocese was preparing

to retire. Like most bishops with whom I had served, I had my thoughts, criticisms, and suggestions about things I would have done quite differently had I been the bishop. All priests have these thoughts. But in the case of the bishop, we all seemed to be speaking these thoughts—with more vitriol than we should have. Instead of mere grumblings about what we would do if we were in charge, clergy friends and I got into the habit of spilling unkind, hurtful words about him. The words tasted like vomit in my mouth; I had gotten used to the taste.

A few weeks before my trip to Spain, I attended a conference that included several sessions on dignity, a word many of us speak with regularity, but likely have a difficult time actually understanding. Or maybe that's just me. During the week-long gathering, the presenter talked about dignity, that essential need of human souls to know they matter and have inherent worth. She also discussed what happens when we feel that we have been shamed, humiliated, excluded, or diminished. Namely, that we react in hurt and anger. We were invited to reflect on times when our dignity had been violated and when we had violated another's dignity.

In our small group, I recalled a gathering right before I came to the conference where several clergy were reflecting on the work of our soon-retiring bishop. While the conversation began with valid commentary, it quickly degenerated into personal attacks on the bishop, and I participated. Disagreeing with an authority figure in the church about his viewpoints on the full inclusion of gay men and lesbian women is a fair criticism. Speculating about substance abuse issues, family of origin issues, or anything that presumes we have any idea about the challenges or inner experiences of others in a way that diminishes them is simply mean. That evening, and for many other conversations, I had been mean. Now, with these peers, I looked at the floor.

"I spoke words that humiliated and diminished this man."

No one said anything, as we had all owned times when we

participated in this particularly damaging behavior toward another person or group. Finally, someone spoke.

"The gift is we can change the conversation."

So I did. When I arrived back in Louisiana, I stopped by the bishop's office. He was surprised to see me, I think, and even more surprised as to why.

"I need to apologize to you. I have said things about your leadership and you personally that are diminishing and shaming and hurtful. I am sorry." I went on to name things I had said or with which I had agreed, without protest. He listened, then leaned forward on his desk, and said, "Thank you."

We talked for a while, not so much about my apology, but about what he would look forward to in retirement. He asked me how I was doing. I told him I was fine. He nodded at me and said, "You are a good and gifted priest."

I thanked him. He repeated his statement again, and said to me, "Do not forget that, even when others might want you to forget."

"I won't," I said, a bit confused about why he seemed so certain of the words he spoke.

As I walked down the street to my car, I explored the surprise in my soul. I rather expected the bishop to at least express disappointment or anger, but he simply expressed grace. Not all apologies end in a restored relationship or a new beginning. Sometimes the damage is so critical that the best we can hope for is a tremendous learning experience so we hopefully avoid such a nuclear meltdown again. My time with the bishop was healing for me. Spiritually, I had vomited up words that I was speaking that did not belong in my soul, words I spoke not so much because I believed them, but more so because others spoke them, and joining the gang of priests felt easier and safer than standing alone. I had spoken truth, admitting what I had said, recognizing how I had violated his dignity.

In that moment, when I thought I was standing alone,

apologizing to a man for things I suspect he may never have known I said, I heard my voice shake and felt very afraid of what he might say. My fear disappeared when his hand touched mine. I looked at him, and he smiled. His gestures communicated a gentle grace, the grace of forgiveness and the grace of being heard. In that moment of awareness and apology, a small piece of my soul moved and shifted. At the time, I didn't perceive its importance, but the minute shift had an impact that would have significant consequences for my self and soul as a woman and as a priest.

None of that would begin tangibly to surface for months, and I was ready to walk on Spanish soil. I arrived in Barcelona mid-November. I ate tapas and drank amazing Spanish wine and wandered for hours and hours in Catalan churches and art museums. The months before my trip, I had studied Spanish; I wanted to learn enough to get myself unlost, to order food, to find the restrooms, and to chat with docents.

St. Paul is a popular saint in Spain, so I was surrounded with images of the saint of the parish where I worked in this land where I was visiting. He was, according to scripture, quite a troublemaker among early Christians until God got his attention by blinding him. Then he became probably the most successful early Christian missionary.

I wandered through the elegant images of Paul carved in stone and painted on altar pieces, and I could have given a rat's ass about seeing them. St. Eulalia resonated more with me. Carvings of her martyrdom decorate the walls of the Catedral de Barcelona. I stood in front of a carving of a woman being tossed into a barrel filled with glass or knives or something else horrible and scanned my church history memories, trying to figure out exactly who this particular saint was. I finally asked a docent, who said she was Eulalia, patron saint of Barcelona. I had never heard of Eulalia.

Eulalia lived in then-Roman Barcelona in the early fourth century, when the Emperor Diocletian decided to have yet another persecution of Christians. Eulalia, refusing to recant her Christian faith, was subjected to thirteen tortures, including being put in a barrel filled with horrible sharp things and rolled down a hill, having her breasts cut off, being crucified on an "X"-shaped cross, and finally decapitated. Legend says that when she was decapitated, a dove flew from her neck.

"Very sad," the docent said. "A girl mutilated because of what she believed."

"A girl mutilated because she refused to conform to the authority," I observed.

The docent nodded, then went on to tell me that the remains of Eulalia resided in the crypt, which was constructed from part of the original chapel on the site.

Thirteen swans reside in the gardens of the Catedral, recalling Eulalia's thirteen tortures. The swans were elegant and lovely, quite an odd symbol for mutilations. The swans, I read in my guidebook, were an early form of alarm. Swans make a horrible noise when disturbed by someone looking to steal or do other criminal activity. Thus, the guard wakes and protects the sacred space. Thirteen elegant symbols of a woman's mutilation, serving as an alarm.

Later I was intrigued by Gaudi's light. A day at the Sagrada Familia, Gaudi's unfinished cathedral masterpiece, was filled with light and abstractness. The interior of Sagrada Familia is filled with carvings that sing of creation. The stained glass is both clear and colored, allowing just the light to form the art. Gaudi had no need or desire to manipulate the light and colors of glass into tightly formed pictures that assumed the images of God, Jesus, and almost every other saint. Those images are human constructs, and Gaudi stripped away the constructs simply to allow light.

On one of my final evenings in Spain, I found a dark corner in a chapel of one of the many churches in Madrid and sat with my journal. Eulalia, a girl mutilated for her beliefs, remembered by elegant swans that guard her church. Gaudi, who envisioned a church with winding and twisting forms filled with unbounded light. I paused in my writings, listening to the priest quietly pray night prayers. Liturgical language is similar, regardless of the native tongue. A prayer card I tucked in from a trip to London fell from my travel journal. As the priest chanted the evening psalms, I read the prayer written by John Henry Newman.

> *Lead, kindly, Light, amid the encircling gloom,*
>
> *Lead thou me on;*
>
> *The night is dark, and I am far from home,*
>
> *Lead thou me on.*
>
> *Keep thou my feet; I do not ask to see*
>
> *The distant scene; one step enough for me.*[3]

Breathing in the incense, I heard the priest come to the end of his prayers. "Amen," I repeated after his voice echoed through the ancient stone walls. I sat silently for a while, in the darkened chapel, watching the votive candles flicker. I allowed my pen to draw random swans on the margins of the page as I thought about the mutilations I felt. No one singular deep mortal wound, but thousands of tiny cuts were letting my soul bleed out in drops.

In the dark, I felt safe. I felt safe enough to name some of the mutilations—I didn't feel valued or heard; I didn't feel authentically me; I didn't feel safe. I prayed Newman's words, then quietly chanted the Magnificat. I would return to Louisiana tomorrow, to my life in a parish that felt very much not my life, but the life dictated to me to live. My song would stay in this space and moment, for now.

Night is dark, and I am far from home.

---

3 Hymn 430, The Hymnal of the Protestant Episcopal Church of the United States of America, 1940 (New York: The Church Pension Fund, 1963).

24

The Zombie of God

I N THE DEEP SOUTH, BAD ju-ju turns living souls into the walking dead. Not intentionally, mind you. I'm quite certain that people don't voluntarily offers up their souls to be part of the living dead. Zombies are made by external forces. Another zombie bites them and, poof, zombie. Several people had gnawed on my soul and consumed parts of it, leaving me a zombie in my own life.

God's zombies, however, are another matter. God happily uses everything at her disposal to coax us into death so we can return to life, even the damned unpleasant stuff. God's economy doesn't waste much in life, like the legends of certain earthy tribes, who wasted nothing of the animals they killed. The meat was eaten, the hide was used for clothing, the bones were tools, and the fat became soap. Every part of the animal was valuable and useful. Other more advanced materials have replaced bones for tools, so we cast off the skeletons. Fat is bad for us, so out it goes too. We only like the finest meat; the rest is left as a decaying carcass.

I, in my high-mindedness, find certain things distasteful. Certain organ meats are gross. I remember my grandmother eating scrapple for breakfast, which was some mixture of eggs and brains.

Yep, I did not eat scrapple.

My soul only wanted the finest meat. I did not want the decaying carcass. I didn't want the distasteful part of life, that part that can't be saved by anyone else, but is discovered only by delving into my own wounds to find the deepest graces of God. I wanted only to see the pleasant aspects of life, of priesthood, and of who I was. And I wanted to stay there. After all, who doesn't?

Without depth, however, there isn't much for the soul to ground in. When nice becomes the most important aspect of my personality, when who others want me to be overtakes the desires of my own self, when the path I'd been walking was one dictated by someone else, my soul decided to wander away.

She wanted mud and instinct; she wanted her heart to sing. She wanted to pray with all of who she was, not just repeat words in a formal prayer book with no thought to the soul of the worship. She wanted to be known for who she was, good and bad. Most importantly, she wanted to be heard and not ignored or bullied. God agreed with her. And when the soul wanders, the body is less than.

Thus, why sleep well? Why gain weight? Just fade away. Just become a holy, obedient little zombie who celebrates the Eucharist, preaches the good sermons, hangs out with the guys, and says how much she loves her job.

Zombies don't have much energy for delving into the truth of authentic self.

God, however, is really big into the truth, that thing that will set you free only after it breaks you and pisses you off or any number of things that are so, so very uncomfortable, like wearing a pair of underwear that keeps riding up with each step. I had no taste for the truth. I kept repeating that I was still grieving the deaths of three people, that I was in a low time in my job, and that things would get better. I had done some things in my new position that nourished me in small, temporary ways. They were easy salves for my soul that offered me some transitory relief, but they didn't heal the deep pain.

My attempts at the easy fixes weren't done. I looked for one last distraction. A guy I knew from HIV/AIDS work called about an article I'd written and, during the course of our chat, asked about the National Championship football game. I was happy to have someone who wanted to hear my enthusiasm about Alabama's decisive victory. I grew up an Alabama fan. I've seen my father cry three times—when both of his parents died, and when legendary Alabama football coach Bear Bryant died. My family takes football seriously.

I told Dan how I had almost to act like it wasn't important to me because I lived in the middle of enemy territory, also known as Louisiana. He laughed. He grew up a Kentucky fan, which means basketball was his sport of choice. We talked about his year in South Africa. I laughed when I talked with him, and I liked feeling that lightness. He called two nights later, and we talked, which led to regular phone calls about daily life. He was a good listener to my ennui, and I enjoyed having this new thing in my life. His job required him to travel quite a bit, mostly in the Kentucky-Ohio area, but he talked one evening of an upcoming trip to Memphis.

"My stepbrother's getting married there next month," I said.

"Why don't I go with you?"

I paused. Granted, my wiser self found this to be a bit sudden for someone. A guy I'd been talking to for a couple of weeks just invited himself to a family wedding. Another part of me was excited. I would have a date to this family event, where I often felt very alone in the midst of relatives who did not understand my life or vocation nor seemed very interested in asking.

So I said yes.

The guy who was good on the phone did not translate into real life. He talked incessantly about his life in South Africa, never missing an opportunity to relate any given event to South Africa.

Lunch at Steak and Shake? They have hamburgers in South Africa. Driving to Graceland? Paul Simon used South African singers on his *Graceland* album. Bright sunny day in Memphis in March? The sun shines in South Africa. It was the kind of commentary that would have been really funny if I'd had another date and he was the awkward family friend that danced with himself at the reception. And I had been slightly drunk. But no, he was my date who acted like the awkward eighth-grade boy who took me to my first dance, except that eighth-grade boy made me laugh. And had never been to South Africa.

Dan simply made me wonder if I was capable of making a good decision at all. How had I so misjudged our phone conversations? At the end of the long weekend that included several phone calls to Brad and Mary about what a disaster this whole date had been and how the next man I took to a wedding would be the one I was marrying at said event, Dan announced to me that his heart was not in it.

I had no idea what "it" was, other than a date to a wedding. I wondered how this all felt so overwhelming. Part of me was relieved; part of me was angry; part of me was sad. He still wanted to be friends. I wanted never to see him again, but I was more scared of losing the one thing that had given me something to smile about in recent weeks. So I agreed, and he left.

When I returned to work, I was completely zombie-fied. I could easily attribute my walking dead state to Dan not being the knight on the white horse to save me from my life, but I knew this decay was deeper. What rot I would have to dig through over the coming months was beyond me at the moment, but through the next few weeks, I was assaulted with unhelpful advice, all of which I swallowed. My zombie self didn't have much differentiation between helpful advice and assaultive meddling. Some clergy with whom I worked said I should work harder at being a priest; that Dan was certainly gay, which is why he dumped me; and that I probably needed Prozac because I was depressed. Other coworkers opined that I had father issues and I was having a crisis of faith and/or a crisis of vocation.

The words felt manipulative and disingenuous. Hearing my rector say that he just wanted the old Laurie back implied, to me, that my entire existence was to make him feel okay. By not being "okay," I was disturbing the perfect balance at St. Paul's of the clergy gang of friends, I thought, which made me feel even worse. I wasn't even sure who the old Laurie was, but I knew enough about journeys to know that you never end them the same person you were at the beginning. I was not going back, only forward. I felt slightly heartbroken that with this journey forward, I would disappoint my rector, and I knew I would pay a price for that as I experienced my confidence, reputation, and self being systemically undermined by people I called friends.

Even in the realization of my current vocational and personal sadness at St. Paul's, I did reflect on the times I had laughed in the company of the clergy. When I was nervous about singing the Eucharist, the other male priests gathered at the altar joked to ease my tension. When one of the clergy had knocked over the chalice, spilling wine everywhere, we laughed. We even laughed together in sadness when John, preparing to go into the final surgery, was asked his blood type and he replied, "Single malt."

I missed laughing with my fellow clergy, and I grieved how this soul journey that had begun and was far from done may mean the laughter with them may diminish, even end. But to stay the old Laurie so others felt happy would eventually kill me; it was killing me now. Perhaps, however, I could pretend to be the old Laurie, until whatever was wrong was fixed. In this place of death and decay, I wanted desperately to laugh again, so I listened to their advice and believed them.

I believed that I was clinically depressed, even though no one on staff had a medical degree. I believed that if Dan were back in my life, I would feel better. When he called me, which he did with frequency, and told me how important I was to his life, how he saw us holding hands walking down a road together, and how he loved me, I believed he was honest and he really did care about me. I believed I was having a crisis of faith, so if I just focused more during worship or read more books on spirituality, I would be okay. I believed I could still be safe in this place, and I was willing to exist as a zombie to be safe, even with mounds of evidence to the contrary.

My zombie existence began to take a physical toll. I had lost over thirty pounds, and I was four pounds from officially being underweight for my height. I hadn't gotten a full night's sleep in months. I began missing school chapel services simply because I did not have the physical energy to get dressed in the morning. Showering exhausted me. My morning routine took two hours or more so I could rest in between showering, doing my hair, getting dressed, and walking my dog. Zombies don't have much energy for personal hygiene, I guess.

I was sliding into a deep brokenness that scared me. I suspect it scared those who worked with me and my friends who loved me. Perhaps the coworkers' observations were ways to salve their fears or exert some control in a situation that was not theirs to control. Perhaps my rector thought he could save me. Perhaps simply voicing their fears to me instead of trying to fix me would have led to a different outcome that what was to come. But those were choices they did not make.

My friends, especially Brad and Mary, did make the choice to be unsure and honest with me. They told me they wanted me to laugh again and missed my witty sense of humor.

"Are you afraid that I'll hurt myself?" I asked, since one of the priests who had read my latest blog entry had told me in that ephemeral way that "it scared him," yet offered nothing to elaborate.

Mary reread the blog, then had two of her friends and her mother read the entry. "No. I'm afraid you're finally going to have enough of being diagnosed through blog entries and gossip until you throw your prayer book at one of the priests on staff and hurt them."

I laughed.

She asked me what I needed.

"I need someone to listen, not to judge, diagnose, or try to fix. And I need you to trust me."

"I have always trusted you, and you will walk this path and be okay," Mary said. I wasn't sure I believed her, that I would be okay, so I talked about my fears of never laughing again. And she listened.

Over home cooking at Cracker Barrel, she listened. On the phone as I sat on my chapel-porch at night, she listened. Walking through the streets of New Orleans during my weekly visits to that city, she listened.

Brad listened too. He and I talked every day, if only about the fabulous food I had eaten at the new cafe I'd discovered in New Orleans or the latest BBC costume drama we were both watching or how I'd started to go into work through the backdoor so I wouldn't encounter my coworkers who would ask me questions I didn't want to answer like, "How are you doing today?" as if I was the fragile sister just back from rehab. The questions, I felt, weren't about listening, but only fodder for more unwanted and unhelpful advice or to gather information that they could discuss out of my presence.

Both Brad and Mary had walked this path of being broken. Brad, as an openly gay priest in the church, had wounds from bigotry and hate. When his mother died suddenly early in his priesthood, he had wounds from grief. And when his relationship to his long-time partner ended, he had wounds from heartbreak.

Mary's struggles to live fully into her vocation, to end her marriage, and to be a mother were equally wounding, even crushing. Having someone listen who is sitting in the mud and blood of her own life is far more impressive and loving than being lectured to by those who pretend as if they have never been broken or, if they do admit to hardships, quickly tell you how they overcame them to become the super-person they are today.

I do not trust people who have not touched their own wounds, and I was discovering that a sure sign of those souls is their vehement need to fix your wounds quickly and easily. I was beginning to suspect that the need to fix my pain was more about their discomfort with my journey than my healing and well-being.

The resilient and beautiful souls are wounded, and those souls trusted me to wander in the great wilderness of God, even in spite of their fears. Grief expert Elisabeth Kübler-Ross wrote, "The most beautiful people we have known are those who have known defeat, known suffering, known struggle, known loss, and have found their way out of the depths. These persons have an appreciation, a sensitivity, and an understanding of life that fills them with compassion, gentleness, and a deep loving concern. Beautiful people do not just happen." Through the witness of my beautiful, defeated friends who themselves had suffered, I was discovering in my darkness the saving power of listening, sensitivity, and compassion. Unsolicited advice borne out of power and denial of pain does not save anyone; soulful concern borne from one's own suffering and subsequent healing does.

My suffering was a deep brokenness, a thick, dark wilderness far away from the well-manicured stability into the great deep of God. It's foreboding and scary, the place where doubt and fear and not much else seem to be my only companions. Some life events drop us suddenly into the middle of this place quickly, and we wake up one morning enclosed by thick woods, separated from the things of security. Other times, we ease into the woods, step by step, until we are deep within this tomb of darkness. I had taken this route. For the last nine months, I had wandered down the meandering path that just seemed to be there. My steps had not been conscious; in fact, I had simply walked because the path was there. Now the hour seemed very late and the way was clouded, even shrouded, and I realized the path that had gotten me in this place would not lead me out.

This was a moment of terror, for me anyway. I wandered, step by step, until I collapsed in the middle of all the grief and bereft feelings that wrapped around my soul and pulled me to the ground. And there I lay.

Trust me, had I known the path I walked would lead to this spot, I would have taken another road. That's the thing about the road less traveled. It's less traveled for a reason. People generally see the dark woods, the bones strewn around on the margins, and all the other signs that walking this path will be hard and difficult and tearful, and turn around. I apparently ignored these signs. Or maybe my wiser self didn't, and knew the journey was one necessary and absolutely vital for my authentic self's survival.

Either way, I escaped to Mary's for a few days. I tucked my feet underneath me on Mary's new couch. She'd started to buy furniture for her new apartment. I told Mary how I'd heard the rector wanted to put me on permanent sabbatical, which is a nice way of firing someone with pay until she becomes another church's problem when she gets another job.

"Did he say that to you?"

"No, but I've been hearing lots of things lately. I don't even know what to believe anymore. I seem to be the topic of conversation. Even parishioners seem to think I've had a nervous breakdown."

Mary raised her eyebrow. "Is that the current diagnosis? I had no idea so many mental health professionals were on staff at your church." Her tone wed sarcasm and protectiveness. "You seem to be the topic of gossip, not conversation."

Mary added, "Shut down the information superhighway. If people at work are going to take your brokenness and use it against you, stop talking to them," she said, quite firmly. "You have me, Brad, and plenty of people who love you who don't think you are crazy. Talk to us. We will never use your words as weapons."

She was right. Realizing, however, that people you thought were friends defined friendship as you being fun and happy was yet more grief. Friendship for me is a relationship where, when you need to fall on the floor, they just sit with you until you get ready to move. And, when you need it, they'll bring you chocolate.

"Maybe I deserve it."

Maybe I had created all this mess, and I deserved all of this. I wasn't being a good priest in this parish. I wasn't being one of the "gang," like the other clergy were. I wasn't satisfied with a well-paying job at a big parish. Maybe I wasn't being a good friend to the clergy at St. Paul's.

Mary shook her head and took a sip her wine. "Maybe you should just quit fighting God." Her voice was surprisingly steady and sure.

That advice I didn't like. That advice didn't have a quick fix or a book to read. I would rather be having a crisis of faith. Then I could just pray harder and sing a few more hymns. Right?

Unlike the other advice I'd received, Mary's was exactly what I needed to hear, and advice that I knew came from her own pain and struggle of the past year. So I did the only thing I could do at that moment.

I surrendered to God.

And then I cried for about twenty minutes or several hours and said, "I'm just so tired of trying to get out."

"Don't try. The rest of us don't have any better sense of your journey. Just stay lost in the deep of God for as long as you need to be lost. God knows where you are." She handed me a tissue.

So there I was, as the great fish vomited me out onto a strange shore—the place I didn't want to go, until the tomb was ready for me to leave its confines, and until my soul decided to settle back into my skin.

I was lost in the deep of God. I was in that place between death and life, scared and weary.

25

Drawing into Grief

M Y THERAPIST HENRIETTA REPEATED HER question. "How have you grieved?"

I tossed back the usual intellectual answers. I'd cried some, taken a few days off. I'd felt sad. But I was fine, my new favorite answer. Most people don't push on that answer to, "How are you?"

Henrietta, of course, was not most people. Her job was to probe more deeply and ask more questions. She did not seem convinced at my answers to wholly valid questions. In the last year my clergy colleague had died, and my grandmother died, and then my step-father's mother had died very suddenly. And Mary, one of my dearest friends, was divorcing her husband. I had struggled with the weight of the grief and the expectation I perceived among my work colleagues that I be "okay" with the gravity of these losses.

I found myself getting physically sick before going to work. Gaining weight is hard when you're vomiting before leaving the house. My hip was bothering me again. My usual evening runs were almost too painful to make them worthwhile, and the exercises my physical therapist recommended did not seem to be working. I hadn't slept well, if at all, for the past eight or nine months. My nocturnal disruptions began with me waking at about 5:00 a.m. after falling asleep at 2:00 a.m., if lucky.

I do many things in life, but waking up voluntarily at 5:00 a.m. has never been on my list of favorite activities. I love the Daily Office of Morning and Evening prayers, but think saying prayers before 8:00 is simply a disgrace. Evening Prayer at the setting of the sun is much more my style. I'd chalked my new sleeping patterns to middle age. I was, after all, now forty.

By the way, nothing on television at 5:00 a.m. is worth watching.

I shrugged my shoulders. I knew the stages of grief—denial, anger, bargaining, something that I always forget, and acceptance. I checked them off in my mind. I finally admitted I felt a bit off, but couldn't put much more to the word than that.

"Are you journaling?"

I nodded. I'd brought my journal to her, as usual. I read some of the things I'd written in the mornings, as I sat on my chapel porch with coffee, watching the sun rise.

"I feel off, which is a sure sign that I'm wandering down one of those roads less traveled. Or I'm just crazy. All the other clergy I work with seem fine, but I don't feel fine. Right now, I just feel off, like the feeling I have when my clothes don't fit quite right because I've gained a few pounds."

"But you haven't gained weight," she said. "In fact, you keep losing weight." She had a clipped Swiss accent that made her words sound even more serious.

"I guess that's how I'm grieving," I replied.

"What else have you written?"

I read what I wrote two mornings ago.

"Grief is so heavy and uncertain. It is filled with sorrow and emptiness, and we are quite certain sorrow will kill us. We don't speak of grief that often in the world, and when we do, it is in whispered tones. I am grieving those I love. I know they are gone, so I'm not in denial. Maybe I'm bargaining, that I can exchange some of my memories of those I love for feeling okay again. Would we do that, if we could? Would we give away some of our soul so we could feel better?"

I started to read more when she interrupted me. "That sounds very nice, like an essay or sermon."

Her observation was not a compliment.

"I don't want you to write any more. I want you to draw."

I looked at her. I reminded myself I paid for the time I spent with her. "Draw?"

"With your left hand. Get some crayons and paper, and each morning, draw for ten minutes."

"What do I draw?"

"What you feel."

I could feel my anger, actually, seething. Draw? With my non-dominant hand? I was not an artist. I was a writer, and she was taking that away from me.

"Draw!" I said, more angry than I wanted to sound.

"Why are you angry?"

"Because I can't draw! I'm a writer. I got scolded in kindergarten for coloring a person's face purple."

"So draw how you felt as a four-year-old scolded for being creative."

I stared at her for a long time. She met my silence with her profound ability to sit in the midst of that discomfort.

"You want me to draw my way out of grief?"

"No," she said. "I want you to draw your way into it."

My blood ran cold. I had spent the last few months convinced I was working through the stages of grief because of the deaths I'd experienced. My sessions with my therapist had been heavy on the "I'm grieving deaths" conversations. I wanted so badly to tell my therapist that yes, I had grieved, but the offness of my soul said otherwise. What troubled me was the feeling that the grief was not simply about the death of people I loved. I knew that grief.

This was something far deeper, far more complex. This was that journey of the soul that required the one more step into the deep woods that meant the only way to go was forward into the darkness and shadows. Spiritual mystics use many metaphors to represent the deep journey of the soul that all humans are called to undergo. The dark night, time in the desert, dropping into the great deep, and entering into the woods.

I spent most of my adolescence living in rural Mississippi, in the woods. Directions to our home included, "Turn off the paved road." Our house sat on a high hill surrounded by swamps on either side. My father, who could not get far enough away from society, cleared just enough land to build the house. Large trees embraced the edges of our home and were our front, back, and side yards. Other kids played in their backyard. My sister and I were juvenile forest rangers. Rarely in my childhood did I get lost, but I did manage a few forays into the deep swamps where the ceiling of tree branches and leaves shielded the sun and the mud and briars reminded me that straying off the path was always hazardous.

I almost always strayed off the path. I even ditched shoes to feel the mud squish between my toes. Wildness lives off the path, and that's where the best mud for bare feet is as well. Wildness is mine, a part of my soul, of all souls, really, that is wholly authentic. Wildness runs barefooted and colors people's faces purple. And, like most people, my wildness had been slowly constrained by the expectations of life, even the expectations of the church.

Quite contrary, actually, to Jesus, who seemed rather annoyed by those who had the good resumés. He was more interested in the authentic wildness of people, from the men and women who left behind societal expectations to follow him to his own authentic wildness that landed him on the cross.

I ticked off my accomplishments to my therapist. High school cheerleader and valedictorian? Check. Sorority president? Check. Honor societies? Check. Law degree? Check. Priest? Check. Priest in a parish with a million-dollar budget? Check. I had been well-rewarded because of these tangible successes.

"And you needed those. We all do, as our egos develop. Something has to give form to the wildness," she reminded me. "Now, maybe, it's time to trust that your holy wildness is ready to hold its own form."

I sat in silence for several moments. "I have no idea how to do that," I quietly admitted. "I can't remember her."

For the past few months, even years, I'd been the well-behaved, obedient, nice girl priest. I liked the people my rector liked and didn't like the people he didn't like. When I voiced my discomfort about a priest who, in the middle of a clergy gathering, grabbed his crotch and told me to "bite him," I was told not to let people know where you keep your goat. When I suggested that the death of a fellow priest was a traumatic event and perhaps we should talk to a therapist about our grief, I just nodded when the response was, "We get all our issues worked out in seminary." I even forced a laugh when the rector replied to my resistance to try a certain food, that I'd had worse things in my mouth.

I'd laughed as priests slaughtered my dignity. I'd been the good girl as clergy made me feel like a cheap woman. I swallowed the dictates wholly—be the person we want you to be, and all will be well.

Until I was no longer well.

Henrietta's face darkened as I told her these events. "You became the nice girl to survive."

There is a place for the nice girl priest in the world, but she was one small aspect of me who had been running the show for far too long. The more authentic part of my soul had simply had enough. When she had tried to speak, I had ignored her. Like Eulalia's swans, the wild part of my soul recognized a dangerous environment and started making noise. She knew that when a person expresses discomfort or voices hopes and dreams, those words should be heard and not discounted. She knew that certain behavior was not joking, but harmful and inappropriate. She knew that the stories of priests who were tossed away as "crazy" or "troublemakers" were warning stories told just in case I decided to step off the dictated path and run wild in the mud. She knew that how people treat their enemies is simply a less-edited way of how they treat their friends. When she had tried to yell, I just turned up the volume on the lyric that kept repeating: "I am fine."

So the authentic wildness of me began to die. And physically, I was sliding away into nothing, pound by pound. My grief was about all I had lost through loved ones who had died, and my grief was about my own soul who was dying because in my desire to be safe, in my hope to believe that the church was a safe place, I had exchanged the life of my soul for security.

"Maybe my rector is right, that I'm just depressed."

Henrietta sighed again. She didn't have much use for the diagnosing skills of people who diagnosed others without years of their own therapeutic work. "Oh, I think you are depressed."

I looked at her, mildly hoping the next sentence would be a quick-fix prescription other than drawing with my left hand.

"Another Jungian therapist observed that when women are depressed, they need to find out why they are angry, and they need to give that wild anger freedom. From all you have told me, you have many reasons to be angry."

I looked at the floor and twisted my watch on my bony wrist. I took a deep breath and said, just barely above a whisper. "I have many reasons to be angry."

26

Holy Week

I SAT IN MY CAR AND SOBBED.

I do my best crying in my car. It serves as that private place I often need when my heart is breaking, but a public ugly cry might not be the most appropriate reaction. When one is the pastoral presence to a family who has just had a loved one die, breaking down into sobs so that they will then feel compelled to care for you isn't so helpful. So I've learned to take a few deep breaths, say what the sacred moment deems be said, if anything (sometimes the most sacred words aren't words), and be present for as long as needed.

Then I walk to my car, sometimes from the family home, sometimes from the hospital. I sit in the driver's seat and cry. I cry because my soul absorbs the sadness and grief from the emotions of others in these moments. I cry because many times, I love the person who has died too. He or she was a beloved parishioner or friend or family member, and I feel that vacant space. I cry because all of the losses I've felt in my life are still there. Grief is annoying that way—she never wholly goes away, and tug on the right threads, and there she is again. I cry in my car because it's my space between. Too often, I leave a particularly emotional situation, ranging from death to a very difficult pastoral conversation, and have to zip my little self to a meeting to plan the Senior High Summer Camp program or talk about the Episcopal Church Women's Easter Tea. Clergy often have to flip emotional switches on and off in ways which are not helpful to our souls, so we cope how we can at the moment. So I cry in this space between someone's profound grief and another's profound excitement.

But now, now I was crying because I was angry, furious even. Leaving the church after the celebration of the Great Vigil of Easter generally leaves me filled with awe and joy. Not this time. This time, I walked away from the Vigil feeling angry.

The Great Vigil of Easter is the culmination of the Triduum, one three-day service during Holy Week, the week Christians commemorate the final days of Jesus. It is one of the busiest times of the year for many clergy with services on each day. This year, it also coincided with the anniversary of John's death, which would lead to the anniversary of my grandmother's death and the anniversary of my stepgrandmother's sudden death. Just to add to the stress, my stepfather was beginning the first of two serious surgeries for blood clots in his legs.

My memories of celebrating Holy Week in the Episcopal parishes where I was a lay person, a seminarian, and a priest in Alabama were powerful. We spent weeks planning the liturgy, giving due effort to the intimacy that is gathering with Jesus on Maundy Thursday as he shares the bread and wine with us and washes our feet; the stark power on Good Friday as we watch him be killed because of our demands; and the stasis of Holy Saturday as all of creation waits.

Then we celebrate the Great Vigil of Easter, hands down my favorite service of the Christian year. Its symbolism exists in layers. The Vigils that take my breath away begin outside in the darkness of night, with the people gathered. Then the New Fire is lit, blazing ferociously as we light the Paschal Candle, a large candle that symbolizes the light of Christ in the darkness.

After praying together, we as a community process into a darkened church and hear the Exsultet, an ancient song proclaiming the beauty and mystery of the resurrection. We are all standing in the dark together, listening to the beauty of a single human voice, seeing the light of a single candle.

I sat on my chapel-porch the evening of Good Friday, drinking a cup of tea, allowing myself to feel the weight of this week. Somehow I was supposed to preach the joy of the resurrection while I myself felt stuck in the tomb. I had been living in Holy Saturday for months, that space between the actual drama of crucifixion, but certainly not at resurrection. I was in the tomb. Stasis. Existing but not alive.

I'd never paid much attention to Holy Saturday, the day between Christ's Good Friday crucifixion and Christ's Easter Sunday resurrection. It is indeed a part of Holy Week, but not one that gets too much energy. Many churches do not have a Holy Saturday service. It is the shortest Holy Week liturgy in the Book of Common Prayer, and we essentially skip over it and breeze from crucifixion to resurrection.

I can understand. The process of decay, of rotting, of allowing what is no longer living fall away, is quite distasteful and actually just gross. We are uncomfortable with the unresolution that is Holy Saturday. It is neither an end nor a new beginning; it is the space of waiting. Waiting is not a strength for most of us. One trip to the department of motor vehicles proves this truth. Waiting is part of God's holiness. The waiting of Holy Saturday must precede the resurrection.

I hate waiting.

God works at God's own pace, and I was learning to trust the slow work of God. I was also discovering that those who are more uncomfortable than I with waiting were trying very hard to push me into the light of the resurrection, even though they were just speculating about the light at the end of the tunnel that had not yet formed.

I was drawing with my left hand. Most of my drawings into grief were abstract lines and shapes, until several days after Mary's suggestion that I get lost with God, I drew people, all with purple faces. Then I drew a plant, which surprisingly looked like a plant. I drew a few images from my dreams—a dark-haired woman looking at a group of church buildings, a red book on a table. I drew a picture of Dan throwing a net on a woman. She was caught, prey to be consumed.

Dan called regularly. He said I was one of his closest friends. I felt like he was an addiction. Sometimes I had the emotional strength to ignore his drug of attention. Other times I answered the calls. Conversations usually included his talking about his former girlfriend who I suspect was never so former, even when he was the worst wedding date ever, and his telling me how much he loved me. I would hang up and burst into tears, ashamed that I let him rent free into my soul again.

When I saw he was calling on Good Friday, I figured I might as well continue the grief and misery of this day and answer the phone. As usual, he acted as if we were the best of friends. As usual, I wondered when I would finally have the strength never to speak to him again.

He asked about the Good Friday services. I told him they'd been fine.

"Are you preaching?"

"The Vigil."

He proceeded to tell me what my sermon ought to contain. Somewhere in our talks, I'd decided that Dan was one of those people who talked with great frequency about being called to the ordained ministry, but didn't actually want to do the hard self-examination to be ordained. So he lived vicariously through me, and I let him, for now.

"Hey, I was in Lexington last weekend on business, and I went to an Episcopal church that's looking for a new rector."

"Kentucky?" I asked. "And this would have to do with me, why? I'm not looking for a job."

"Why not? You're not happy where you are. So go somewhere else."

I shook my head. I had put him into the category of people who were giving me hurtful and useless advice. "Look, I have to go."

"We'll talk later?" he asked.

I hung up the phone and drew. Surprisingly, drawing gave me something to do with these emotions that I couldn't verbalize. A large woman holding lightening bolts appeared, surrounded by reds, greens, purples, yellows, and blues. I looked at my finished image, then went back to thinking about my sermon.

The next evening, I stood in the back of the church, ready to begin the Vigil. The Vigil at St. Paul's foregoes the gathering outside, and we light the Paschal Candle with some matches (or did that year). The Exsultet was beautifully sung, and the Vigil began. I was preaching the Vigil this year. The power of the liturgy is actually enough of a sermon, but the rector did not agree. So I preached.

One place my authentic voice had not faltered was my preaching voice. In the past month, she had burrowed down into the darkness and found some amazing sermons that surprised me. Her voice had also found an outlet through essays on the blog. This Vigil, I became the voice of Mary Magdalene.

Or I let her share my voice. I talked about sitting at the graveside of this person I loved, after having watched him suffer and diminish and fade from human life. I reflected on that feeling of wondering what I could have done to prevent this, to change this. We all know that place, I said, the place of regret when things turn out badly. We all know that place where we wonder, "Why?" I shared the empty power of grief, where you wished you had listened more closely to the stories, you had said words of thanks and love more often, and you had one more hour. Just one more hour, to break bread together again.

"Imagine that grief," I asked the congregation. "Go back in your souls, remember the person you loved, still love, and still miss. Go to their tomb. Sit with Mary there. Because that's where she is at this moment."

I invited those gathered in the darkness to that place, that silence, and that pain. I noticed several people with faces streaked with those silent, elegant tears.

"And now imagine that person greeting you, reminding you that love never goes away and that death is not the end."

More silence.

"Imagine, in your deep darkness of loss and grief, that you see the light of hope and of love. And feel in your soul the mixture of grief, fear, and joy of Mary, when she heard, 'Why do you look for the living among the dead?'"

I walked to the Paschal Candle.

"Why do you look for the darkness when there will always be light? Will you, will I, join Mary and look for the living?"

"Will we stand in that place where grief, love, loss, and hope blend together in the moment of resurrection?"

At the reception following the Vigil, several people complimented my sermon. One of my fellow clergy said it was the most touching Easter sermon she'd ever heard. Another one said he couldn't hear it, so he was checking baseball scores on his smartphone instead. Others told me of the people they imagined— spouses, partners, children, friends. They shared funny stories and regretful moments. They said they had never thought of the moment of resurrection as one where sadness and joy are wed together. I resisted the urge to explain my theology of thin places. They thanked me for my words and my voice and for making the moment at the empty tomb so very real for them.

I always feel uncomfortable with compliments about my sermons. I've preached enough to know that the words aren't wholly mine, but shared with God. And I never preach a sermon that I don't need to hear. My voice was there, full and authentic. The voice of grief and weariness preached and had something to say.

While I was eating another deviled egg, because in the South you cannot celebrate Easter without deviled eggs, the rector told me how many people had come to him and complimented my sermon.

"Thanks," I said.

He continued to say that had I not gone through such a hard time in the past year with so many deaths and all the other hardships, I could not have preached a sermon like that.

I smiled and said, "Yes, I suppose so."

I eased over to get another glass of punch, then slipped out of the reception. As I drove home, I felt an emotion I hadn't felt in quite a while.

I felt anger. I relived what the rector had said, and I felt even more anger.

How dare a person of faith suggest that God would inflict three deaths, a tragic relationship, a friend's divorce, and my stepfather's surgeries just to get a good sermon for Easter? If that is God, I'm done with Christianity.

But that wasn't God. That was the theology of my rector. His words sounded like a glib remark to rush me out of Holy Saturday right into Easter, ready or not. They felt dismissive to me, as if my grief and struggles of the past year were merely an advanced class in preaching.

In my calmer moments, I may have understood his comment as a poorly stated thought along the lines of "Isn't it comforting to know that you can take the crushing experiences of the past year and find inspiration for a sermon?" I, however, was not calm. I was angry.

The anger I felt scared me. She was dark and brooding, drank her bourbon straight, and knew how to use a knife to protect herself. She had been waiting for a very long time to take the stage, so

I quickly ushered her back into the wings. She, however, refused to be ushered off, so she stood firm and screamed, "Notice me! You have many reasons to be angry!"

And I let her stay. I was angry. I felt the anger, rage even, swirl in me and finally get that last deep breath of holy energy she needed to burst forth into life. And in these moments, I'm really, really glad I'm not in human company or near something that can be used as a weapon.

Anger is powerful. Anger lives in the deepest part of our souls. Most women, and certainly nice Southern girls like me, are warned about anger and how "unpleasant" it is in women. "Nice girls don't get angry," one of my aunts said to me. I began to wonder if Jesus woke up in the tomb angry. We don't get that commentary from any of the Gospellors. I suspect his first reaction was shock. But after that, did he think about all he'd been through, see the deep wounds in his hands and feet and side, and think, "WTF?"

I am not that holy, so I sat in my car in the garage of my condominium, and I was angry. And I needed to be angry. When one wakes from the experience of her soul's crucifixion and death, anger is an understandable response. I was not dead. I was not a zombie. I was angry.

So I cried. And yelled. And beat my fists against the dashboard. I tore some papers scattered on the passenger seat into shreds, and ripped the shreds into confetti. And I yelled at God.

I wanted to know why I had put up with being diminished and constrained by the church for so long. I wanted to know why my grief was dismissed by priests who I expected to be willing to let me grieve. I wanted to know if the bishop was right, that I was being bullied. I wanted to know why I hadn't yelled at my fellow priests to stop making crass comments to me, why I hadn't said "STOP!" to the things that slit my soul in the name of "friendship." I wanted to know why, why, why to questions that my anger wouldn't even allow me to form into words. I screamed so loudly my voice flipped up into octaves only dogs could hear. I just screamed that primal scream with no words. I let my tears wail and wail and rage and rage.

I screamed more with no words, just a deep, soul-searing scream. I took another deep breath, ready to scream and rage again, but his time, words formed.

Why do I have to settle?

Why do I have to settle for being treated as a kid sister? Why do I settle for smiling at an inane comment about a good sermon? Why do I have to settle for laughing at jokes I find offensive and degrading to me as a woman? Why do I have to settle for conforming to my rector's idea of ministry instead of discovering what kind of priest God called me to be? Why do I have to settle for the trappings of importance, power, and significance instead of falling in love with the very essence of my created being, naked of everything? Why do I have to settle for who others think I should be?

And I stopped screaming. I sat in stunned silence, snot smeared over my cheeks, eyes dragon-fire red, and my hands shaking from the fury.

Why do I have to settle?

What? In all that anger and rage, THAT was the question? Not, "Why is my heart broken by people I thought loved me?" Not, "Where is my joy?" Not, "How have I gotten myself almost put on permanent sabbatical?"

Nope. Nothing like that. Just, "Why do I have to settle?"

The question was so honest and shocking that I stopped screaming and wailing, midscream and midwail. Just stopped. And sniffed. I smeared some tears away and did that little stutter breathing that we professional cryers do.

And then I heard God answer me.

"Why do you settle?"

That really stopped my rage, which had calmed to a swirling anger.

"Oh."

Always a proper response to the Holy One who has just poured your own issues over your soul like ice water.

"Oh."

Evelyn Underhill wrote that "Oh" would be the most commonly heard word in heaven. It is the word that means we have been stopped in our tracks by something wholly unexpected, but not terrifying.

"Oh, the delicious chocolate is low-fat?"

"Oh, God doesn't expect me to be perfect?"

"Oh, God wants to know why I settle?"

And in the ending of my time in the tomb, I listened. I listened to myself and the anger that needed a voice. I listened to the pain of my body and soul. I listened to God asking me why I settled.

I began to admit that I had settled. I had acquiesced to words and behavior from fellow clergy that diminished me as a woman. Jokes about my breasts or what I had put in my mouth were degrading, not funny. Comments that women were unfit to be priests from parish rectors that were met with silence from fellow clergy were diocesan-permitted misogyny. I had swallowed the lie that the significance of titles and pay and size of one's church made me special. I had settled for simply existing for the comfort and fun of others, refusing to listen to the voice of my own soul who had her song to sing. And when I had started to give her a voice, I had settled for believing that that voice was crazy and suspect, so I should ignore her and settle for the old Laurie.

The angry part of my soul with a criminal record and too many tattoos who lives in the sketchy part of my soul sat down for a drink with the nice girl. Anger poured a stiff drink, which made the nice girl shudder, then smile after she took a sip. They started to figure out how to end this settling habit and to begin living a bit more authentically.

During the week after Easter day, when most clergy take the week off, I began thinking about what a call to another church might look like. I was scared that I was being reactive, that I wasn't in a grounded place to explore another job. I also realized that simply exploring was not a commitment. I looked at the website for the church Dan had mentioned. While I didn't want to admit he might have given me some good advice, Mary reminded me that even a broken clock is right twice a day. The church had modern architecture and an overwhelming website filled with more information than I could digest. I gave up and called the diocesan deployment officer in charge of taking names of those clergy interested in serving as priests in the diocese of Lexington.

I had no expectations that the diocesan deployment officer would quickly respond to my cold call. Kathryn, the deployment officer, had other ideas. I told her I was exploring the possibility of a new call, and she asked me several questions about my resumé history. Then, as an afterthought, she asked me if I liked football, given that I was from Alabama.

I told her I loved football. Kathryn's father had been a football coach, and we began to talk. And talk. And talk. We talked about life in the church. We talked about being single in the church and being a woman in the church. I directed her to my blog address, and she told me she was already a fan.

Then she asked me, "What kind of church are you looking for?"

I took a deep breath. Anger and the Nice Girl opened their mouth and spoke. "I am tired of settling. I want a parish that lets me sing my song."

I expected Kathryn to politely take my information and tell me she'd get back to me. Most clergy respond with concrete details—the number of services, the amount of the budget, the type of programs. I just wanted a parish that would let me sing my song while they sang theirs.

Instead, she said, "How wonderful. Tell me more."

I told her my whole story. How I had been so hurt by the parish in Mobile, how I had wanted so much to be safe in the church, so when the rector of St. Paul's talked about how he protected his clergy, who were also friends, I felt safe. Until I didn't. Until through my grief I had wandered into the darkness. Until my clergy friends suggested I was having a nervous breakdown, was incompetent, and the words "permanent sabbatical" had been tossed around, presumably to dispose quietly of the troublesome priest I had become.

"Do you feel bullied?" she asked.

"About a year ago, our then-bishop asked my friend Mary the same thing," I replied.

"That's important information, but you didn't answer my question," Kathryn said. Her response felt kind, not demanding. Like Mary and Brad, her voice sounded filled with trust for whatever of my truths could be spoken in the moment.

"Yes," I whispered. Tears slid down my face.

"I cannot imagine how hard your life must be right now. Let's see what we can do, together."

Before Kathryn and I got off the phone, I had given her permission to share my situation with the bishop of Lexington. I had talked to her about St. Gabriel's, and I had agreed to look at information about a conference she was hosting over Labor Day.

"Sometimes just getting away is the best healing," she suggested. "But think about coming, even serving as a chaplain if you feel like it. I'll send you an e-mail."

I was impressed that she was actually suggesting, not demanding something of me. I hadn't heard the words that implied I had permission to say yes or no to something in the institutional church in far too long. I had become so used to taking orders and repeating dictates that I felt unsure about how to discern what I wanted to do.

When I got off the phone, I felt Anger and Nice Girl lift their glasses in a toast. That, for me, felt hopeful.

27

Broken Truth Found in the Graveyard

I N THE MIDST OF MY wasting away to nothing, finding no joy in my vocational life, and being angry as a wasp at times and at other times being fearful of my anger, a friend was being ordained in another denomination and invited me to join him on retreat in a old monastery in the middle of nowhere in Pennsylvania.

My response was pretty much a shoulder shrug. Why not? What could happen?

As a rule, looking at God and asking, "What could happen?" is the ultimate in a foolish dare. God seems to like challenges and will take almost any inroad to our lives. My experience is that retreats are often God's way of handing me a holy shovel, moving me in front of my pile of shit, and saying, "Dig."

Messy, smelly, sweaty, and distasteful work if done right. Even less fun in old monasteries. Old monasteries are great for discomfort of body and soul. The beds aren't that comfortable, but since I wasn't sleeping anyway, I didn't mind that much. The food is high-carbohydrate, mostly non-rabbit food, but since I was dropping weight, anything was helpful, even food that has apparently not been in the same room with any sort of flavoring or even a bottle of Tabasco.

When I initially planned to go on retreat, I thought my biggest and only problem was grief. I had experienced three deaths in a short period of time. I was at the year anniversary. Yep, that's what I needed to do. The logic was right. Life seemed to be fine until something happened, so start tracing your way back down the road to see when the something happened. From the vantage point of my reflection until that point, that was the wrong turn. So I would just process my grief.

A very intellectual approach. So I said my little narrative prayers and asked God to show me the way through this grief. After that scary and holy flash of anger at Easter, I realized the grief was deep, and God handed me a shovel.

I did need to grieve. My years in ministry remind me that grief is never a done process, however much we might like it to be. We do not easily slip through the stages of grief as if they are way stations that simply slow our journey through life. Grief is a part of our souls that is ripped away, and we spend our lives working with and around that part that is now absent. The longer we live and love and lose those we love, the more grief we acquire, so that each subsequent loss just adds to our brokenness. We don't get over grief; we somehow allow it to change us, hopefully for the richer.

Grief is that part of love we would all rather ignore, medicate, and distract ourselves through. When we sign onto this great power called love with our friends and family, we skim the fine print and would rather ignore that aspect that says, "Parts of love will hurt." Grief exacts a price. Love exacts a price. We love people, and then they may leave. Our arms can't hold them anymore. We can't hear their voices. I dream about people who have died, still feel their love, but it is different.

When I arrived at the retreat, I realized I was the youngest person there by a few decades. As I listened to the reflections from the retreat leader, I waited for that magical moment where my heart would be strangely warmed and I would return to okay.

I might as well have wished for a unicorn.

On my walks on the grounds, in between the prayers and the non-rabbit food meals and my nights spent not sleeping, I wondered if I should have listened to all the other voices offering advice about my current life situation and believed them instead of looking at the pile of shit I seemed to keep coming around to, which by and large felt like my entire life at the moment.

Arun Gandhi, the grandson of the famous Gandhi, quotes his grandfather, who said that the most prolific acts of violence in the world are unsolicited advice. For a Southern girl who grew up with the 11th Commandment being, "Thou shalt offer unsolicited advice," this pricked me.

I revisited the advice from my rector who, over and over again, categorized my emotional state as a crisis of faith, even saying, "I was right!" when I told him I was annoyed that the monastery expected us to wear clericals during the retreat. My friends, I thought, would know how much I didn't like wearing clericals when I was supposed to be relaxing and reflecting.

My crisis was not about God. I wasn't any angrier at God than I usually was. Angry at people throwing their opinions about me around, even to parishioners? Angry at not being heard? Angry when my words of vulnerability and doubt were being used to diminish me? Furious is more the word. And devastatingly sad. Much of this anger was rooted in the betrayal by those I thought were friends, and now I was realizing otherwise. Thus, more grief at losing the laughter and trust of these relationships.

One night I wandered into the chapel after I had lain in bed for an hour upon waking up sometime after 4:00 a.m. When I realized I wasn't going back to sleep, I decided to sit in holy space. Apparently, the abbot didn't sleep much either. He and I had chatted briefly over the course of the retreat. He was sitting in a pew, eyes closed. When I saw him, I immediately stopped and turned to leave. The creaking old wooden floors gave me away.

The abbot looked up.

"I'm sorry. I didn't think anyone was here. I'll go somewhere else."

The abbot waved his hand to me to come back in. "This is God's space, not mine. Come sit."

I joined him in the pew. We sat in a silence that felt awkward to me.

He spoke. "I remember when I first came here, years ago. Probably before you were born."

I laughed.

"I come here to say prayers at night. For those people who have talked with me, for those who need healing, and for those who have died. I often end up remembering those brother monks who prayed with me who have died. My friends. I still miss them."

I just nodded. I wasn't crying, yet, but felt certain that trying to speak and not to cry would be impossible.

"How long have you been a priest?"

"Eight years," I said, and started crying. "It's been a hard year."

I started telling him about those who had died, and how tired I was of missing them and feeling sad. How I was starting to wonder how deep this grief went, and when would I start to feel better. "I feel like I'm the crazy one at my church because I'm grieving."

"I wonder why that is."

I fished around in my pockets for a tissue and wiped my nose. "I don't know."

"My experience is that we aren't good at grief. It scares us, so we avoid it, and those of us who deal in death are exceptional at avoiding the pain of grief. It reminds us that we are broken. We priests are some of the most broken people around."

I breathed deeply, still letting my tears drop silently.

"We in God's service like to think we aren't broken, that we are remarkably strong and can handle anything in our path. We like to think we have dealt with our issues, that we have no tender places, but we are broken and quite messy. Do you know Leonard Bernstein?"

I did, and said I was surprised he did.

"What, you think I don't listen to popular music?"

I managed a faint smile.

"He has a line in a song about our broken places, that that's where the light shines through. Your brokenness is where God is trying to shine through, and that is hard, courageous work to recognize your brokenness."

"My therapist quotes that song to me, but I don't feel courageous. I feel crazy."

"Do you feel that, or is that what you've heard?"

"Both."

"Are you drinking too much?"

"No, I stopped drinking anything months ago, because I don't want to drink to numb myself."

"Are you overeating?"

I shook my head. I decided to omit the losing weight issue right now.

"Are you talking to someone?"

I told him about my therapist and my spiritual director and my dear friends.

"Abusing drugs?"

"Nope. I'm just sad."

"Sad is not crazy. It's sad."

"And I'm sad."

We sat in silence again. This silence felt comforting. The early rays of the sun began easing through the stained glass window on the right side of the church.

"Would you like the church tomorrow night, just you and God? Just a place to be sad?"

I said yes, and I knew exactly what I needed to do in that space and time freely to be sad for the first time in months. "I'd like to pray the Burial Office," I said, "but I don't have a Book of Common Prayer."

"I will take care of that."

Late the next evening, a printed copy of the Episcopal Burial Office appeared on the floor in front of my room. The generosity of an elderly abbot printing page by page the Burial Office of another denomination was simply breathtaking. I took the pages and went to the Marian altar in the church. I talked to John and told him I missed him and love him. I talked to my grandmother and said the same.

I called Mary on my phone, and together we prayed the Burial Office. She began with the anthem.

> *I am Resurrection and I am Life, says the Lord.*
>
> *Whoever has faith in me shall have life,*
>
> *even though he die.*
>
> *And everyone who has life,*
>
> *and has committed himself to me in faith,*
>
> *shall not die forever.*

I prayed the opening prayer: "O God of grace and glory, we remember before you this night our brother John and our sister Dixie. We thank you for giving them to us, their family and friends, to know and to love as companions on our earthly pilgrimage."

I stopped to cry, remembering the many, many people I had buried in my time as a priest with the words of this prayer. When I finished the prayer, Mary read the beautiful words from the Revelation to St. John the Divine, reminding us God will wipe away every tear.

But not right now. Right now I just cried, not because I was weak or had issues or was crazy, but because I was sad. For the first time in months, I simply recognized I was sad, and there was nothing wrong with my sadness. There was nothing wrong with my grief.

Mary prayed when my tears were too great. She continued with the prayers for a vigil, which includes the lovely prayer, "May they hear your words of invitation, 'Come, you blessed of my Father.'"

I gazed at the statues of Mary holding an infant Jesus above the altar. Come, John and Dixie, you blessed of God. When life is done on earth, come gaze upon the Lord, face to face, and taste the blessedness of perfect rest.

Come, those who miss them and are sad, and weep at my altar.

And I did. I cried, and Mary stayed on the phone with me, simply being present in holy silence. After she heard me take a deep breath, she began, "The Lord be with you."

"And also with you."

"Let us pray. Almighty God, Father of all mercies and giver of comfort: Deal graciously, we pray, with all who mourn, especially your daughter Laurie; that, casting all her care on you, she may know the consolation of your love, through Jesus Christ our Lord. Amen."

"Amen," I repeated, and breathed deeply for the first time in months. An elderly abbot and my dear friend Mary had reminded me that sadness was not weak or crazy, just sad. And, in their grace, they had given me the space to grieve how I needed to grieve, not how someone else directed me to grieve.

I offered the Easter blessing. I realized in my soul that my loved ones were home, and the amazing love I shared with them still filled me. I recognized the great irony that John would love my prayers in front of the Marian altar, and my grandmother would be appalled at such a "Romish" thing.

And surely I was done.

But no. Because once I had been allowed to feel the emotions in my soul, I felt more of my soul stir and come to life. Over the next few days, I started to reflect more deeply on why I had to come to a monastery in the middle of nowhere to hear that being sad was not wrong. I was a priest in a church with other priests. We sit with people in their brokenness and meet them there. We hand tissues to those who are weeping, and we have classes in appropriate ways to help people express their grief.

And yet, I was not given that right. I felt judged and punished for my grief and its expression. I felt as if my grief was a disappointment to the clergy with whom I worked. The old Laurie, I guess, was never sad.

On the other end of the spectrum, Dan couldn't hear me talk about my grief enough. He called and left a message during my retreat time, even though I'd asked him not to call for my time away, saying he was there to listen if I needed him. His message didn't feel welcoming; it felt predatory, as if my grief for him was something that fed his appetite of the role of nice and compassionate guy. I was done with being his prey.

I was reflecting, or more accurately, seething, over these incidents when another retreatant joined me in the old graveyard. He made a few nondescript remarks about the gravestones. I replied that the weather was unusually warm this time of year. He asked about my vocational life. I gave him the straight facts, then asked him the same.

We walked and talked some more until he asked, "What makes you happy about where you are?"

I opened my mouth to give the replies I'd been giving for years, and absolutely no sound came out. I'd hoped to say things like, "Well, I work in a large parish with a staff and I love my job."

But my entire throat and mouth were filled with utterly nothing. So I breathed in. And I breathed out. I have rarely in my life been unable to speak.

I opened my mouth to say that I loved the Tiffany windows in the church, but instead, I simply cried. I started to cry and breathe and cry and get really, really angry and cry. I crashed down on the ground, next to a grave with the name partially chipped away from time and the elements, and I rested there, with the bodies of monks, and I cried because my heart finally screamed more loudly than my rational mind and spoke with the tears that my soul had been holding back for far too long.

And I finally spoke: "I am not happy there."

I waited for the world to disintegrate. That's what I thought would happen when I spoke the truth that had been buried under the shit in my soul for far too long. That's why we don't speak our deep truths. We are too fearful that saying them will destroy foundations and, if you have enough deep South codependency, as I do, make other people sad, which I had been reared to believe is the worst sin ever. So we continue to redecorate the living room while never speaking of our alcoholic family member or how the marriage has been dead for years or whatever truth will strip away the layers.

God, however, is more about subtraction than addition. God loves to strip away, apparently. Jesus loses a few followers when he starts his diatribe about telling the rich young man to sell all he has or gives the disciples a packing list for their impending mission trip which consists of not much more than what they can wear. God wants us diminished to our barest souls.

I am not particularly comfortable with this truth, but apparently there is always a time when the perfect storm of bad food, lack of sleep, and bone weariness from holding together all the pretense leaves a girl collapsed in a graveyard realizing her joy has left the building.

I was not happy working at the parish under the circumstances that existed. I could no longer say that all of the clergy were friends with each other when I heard hurtful and upsetting comments that questioned my mental state and my competency. I could no longer deny that those things that brought me passion in ministry were simply not a priority for the rector. I was tired of laughing at comments made by diocesan clergy about the shortcomings of my gender as a priest or how good my breasts looked in a clergy shirt and not hear them for what they were—comments that were harassing and demeaning. I was tired of pretending that all was right with my world when I was losing weight and not sleeping.

I was done with being mutilated by these things, and I was finally hearing Eulalia's swans, squawking and screaming to warn me, to wake me, and to alarm me. And I would start by speaking my truth from my experience in the midst of a graveyard, the place where we gather to say goodbye to that which has died and proclaim the eternal life that is to come.

I had to leave St. Paul's to live.

That was my truth, and that truth would hurt people. The parish I served at that time is a good place filled with deeply spiritual people. Many were a source of joy and laughter for me. In their kindness they shared the joys of life with me. The creativity of many with whom I worked inspired me, and I was deeply sad that I could not be their priest in the leadership environment that existed. Leaving them for another call would be sad.

Dualistic thinking wraps us in the lie of either-or, that something cannot be wonderful for one person and a completely life-draining place for another. But truth is not dualistic; it simply is. My experiences and feelings are mine, and I was weary from having them diminished and dismissed.

I don't know how long I sat in the graveyard. I looked up and noticed my walking partner nudging around some stones with his shoes. He smiled at me.

"Sounds like you need to start considering a new call."

I was thankful he didn't ask me if I was okay; I was tired of that question. Instead, he just said what I'd been avoiding for far too long. He offered his hand and helped me up from the grave. We walked into the chapel for Evening Prayer. We sang the service, again, our little band of retreatants. Then we gathered for dinner, which was four starches and tasteless chicken. Over dinner, my friend Ron and I started talking about our experiences as hospital chaplains that were hysterical to us.

And I laughed.

And the pile of shit suddenly became smaller.

28

I Am Wobbly and Alive

FTER LYING ON THE GROUND in a graveyard and admitting that huge chunks of myself and soul were not with me, that I had sacrificed them to the gods of comfort and the agenda of others and simply not rocking the boat, I realized I was just as far in the deep woods and I was out. In other words, getting up and moving out of the tomb meant I would be going forward into a new place where my footprints had never been before.

Where that would be was anyone's guess, but I knew where I was wasn't it. My present was not my future. While on retreat, I continued to draw. On the final day, I drew another purple person, when one of my purple people suddenly had an open mouth, and I drew lovely green, pink, and blue notes. And I remembered the singular soul truth I had spoken to Kathryn: that I needed to find a place where I could sing my song.

My song, the one God had given to me. Not someone else's song, not his or her agenda or ideas, but mine. Granted, I had no idea what this song would sound like. But God's siren song was reaching deep into my soul, stirring this ancient and new place within me.

God was calling me, and I had moved, scars and all, out of the doorway of the tomb. I was coming back to life and seeing my life, the church, my ministry, and my soul in new ways. What I saw was different because I was different. No one descends with God and comes up the same. The old Laurie was gone. God moves forward and drags those of us too stupid and too courageous along. Because it takes that magical and mystical blend of sheer stupidity and sheer courage to drop into the depths with God. No one sane does this. Just take a look at the Christian mystics, the prophets, the saints. Great women and men, but edging on bat-shit crazy at times.

Sanity and intellectual reasoning convince us to stay put. "All is well," we hear our egos whisper. No need to wonder what if. No need to upset the proverbial apple cart. No need to see what might be waiting deeper in the forest. No need to give up power. Certainly no need to go pushing around on those broken places. Many people stay right at the forest's edge, where they can still see the way out, where they are still in control, where they are still safe, and where the wounds are tightly bound with barbed wire, daring anything to touch them.

But some of us wander deeper into the woods, toward the darkness. I had wandered into this place. That siren song of God that only stupidity and courage allowed me to hear and follow. Following is the real trick, isn't it? All of us hear God calling us to that new place. We can ignore God's call quite well, though. We humans have a knack for turning up the radio to drown out the voice of the Holy. I had turned it up for years, I realized.

Something happens for some of us. Maybe the volume can't be turned up anymore. Maybe we just get tired of listening to the music that is playing, so we finally listen to God's whisper, and we follow. Following God is flat-out dangerous. People should pay attention to the warning signs and quit listening to the Jesus is my Boyfriend music that says a journey with the Holy One is all fun and games.

It's not. Just ask anyone who's been there. Worth it? Yes. Easy? No. Remember Jesus? He got crucified.

Because you will be changed. I had been changed, and I knew I was at the very edge of this newness. And more change would come. The mystics explain that as we emerge from the woods or the deep or the tomb (I actually felt like I'd been in all three), we have new gifts and treasures for the next part of the holy journey, which may or may not be something we expected. Probably not, actually, because if we had expected it, we would have been, well, safe and in control. Nothing changes or grows, not even faith, without sacrifice.

And the story of the journey was mine and mine alone for a while. Why do you think Jesus so often told those who encountered his miraculous self to go away and be quiet? Here I sat, letting the slow work of God take firm root in my soul, and walking until I blinked and stretched some more as my eyes focused on the new vision before me. I listened for my soul's song to grow louder, and I remembered that I was among those stupid and courageous enough to yell "Yes!" to God.

Granted, I was still wobbly, so my "Yes!" was more subdued than perhaps one would expect. I was wobbly, unsure, and a bit wary of this new place, like a newborn colt who is just deciding that four legs are indeed for standing. I didn't really know the view that well, but at least I knew that I was authentically me. The previously chipper and sure-of-herself Laurie was now only a fraction of who I was. The Wobbly One took up much more room. And trust me when I say being wobbly is not a particularly comfortable place to be, all in all.

In a series of moments over the past two months, all that I had accumulated in my life, all the degrees and accolades and titles and pay increases, were stripped by God. I discovered that honesty mattered more than comfort, that roles dictated by others come at a cost, and that speaking truth to authority in the church was as dangerous as early Christians speaking truth to Imperial Rome.

My soul had been mutilated and my spirit had been bullied. The external things that gave me a sense of importance and power were ripped away, and I finally opened my hands and let God take the remnants I didn't need.

I was bare, with nothing left but my broken, wobbly mess of a soul lying on a grave in the middle of nowhere special, Pennsylvania. And I had survived with hope and strength. My broken, wobbly mess of a soul was authentically alive. Alleluia, Laurie had risen.

When I got home from the retreat, the Wobbly One trekked to the mailbox and pulled out two weeks' worth of magazines, catalogues, junk mail, and bills. And one letter: one holy letter inviting me to apply to be the rector of St. Gabriel the Archangel in Lexington, Kentucky.

And I stood just a bit more steady.

29

Death at a Parish

I SLEPT THAT NIGHT IN MY home on my stomach, or I tried to sleep.

Instead, I lay awake and clasped my hands over my heart. Surely that would help, because the wail of its beats was so painful I wondered how it wouldn't fall out of my chest. How had my time at St. Paul's come to this?

The day had started normally enough. I'd gone to the office, done some nondescript priest stuff that involved a few e-mails and reading a book on the Gospel of Mark. Summers are usually slow times in the church, so all those books we clergy-types bought in seminary to stock our shelves so we look like we are well-read get opened in the months between May and September.

Several hours later, I was sitting in my car, crying (because why mess with a good practice). I'd left work immediately when a diocesan staff member told that my days at St. Paul's were numbered and the rector wanted to fire me. When I'd finally cried as much as I could cry in the car, I went into my home and cried some more.

Realizing my grief needed some company, I called Robert, a priest in Texas, and told him of the day. I don't think he could really understand the last four minutes of my words because I was in that ugly cry-trying-to-talk mode. But he heard enough, because after I finished, he simply said, "Laurie, you remember who you are and whose you are."

And then he told me who I was: a beloved child of God with gifts for ministry. He reminded me of the way I sang the Easter preface and laughed at the end, and how he thought all Easter prefaces should end with laughter. He reminded me that my dreams of God from the very beginning of my life were still with me. And he told me whose I was: God's. In his usual humor, he reminded me that being God's did not mean nothing bad would ever happen again, but that I was going to be okay. He made me promise I wouldn't quit and that I would continue to offer myself to discernment.

While all he said was true, and most of my soul heard it, I still wept at the truth that caused me to sleep on my stomach to protect my heart. Somewhere in the gospels, I'm quite sure Jesus said that the truth will set you free, but first it will break your heart, then simply piss you off.

I was in the heartbroken stage at the moment, and had been since after lunch earlier that day, when I'd been skimming a book on the Gospel of Mark, then summoned to a member of the diocesan staff's office, where I'd been told that my boss wanted to fire me for passive-aggressive disloyalty. Or was going to put me on permanent sabbatical. Or dye my hair magenta. Or steal my crayons during recess. The exact details don't matter; what mattered is that I believed all of it and felt hopelessly defeated in that moment.

All that I had hoped to find in the church, all that I had expected in this gathering of the faithful who promised to speak the truth in love finally vanished in that moment. What is so tragic about hearing horrible news about someone with whom you are in relationship, a friend, coworker, or partner/spouse, is the moment when you are aware that you absolutely believe the awful news you've just heard. You don't even pull into the rest stop of "no, surely this is just a misunderstanding."

Nope, you go right to the place of stark naked truth where you realize the relationship is so damaged and broken that there is no way it can continue. Too many threads have become unraveled. Going back is impossible, because I don't have amnesia. Going forward is unlikely, because I don't have amnesia.

We've all received news or gossip or speculation that someone—a friend, a spouse, or partner, or someone—has said or done something that may hurt us, even that has hurt us.

"I didn't know you and your boyfriend broke up. I saw him last night having dinner with another woman. She was cute."

"Oh, Mary was telling someone that you have gained weight."

Yep, those moments where we hear something from someone else about someone we care about. In my world, the bitchy friend who has shared said information falls quite neatly into two categories: those great friends who are loyal to you and will tell you even the most painful things because they love you and those people who tell you things like this to stir shit up. The former will sit with you in the mess of the bomb they have just delivered. The latter will run to the person about whom they've just told you and tell them how hurt or angry you were to set off yet another bomb.

The former people remind me God loves me. The others remind me that God loves people I don't like. The mad bombers also make me pray more, because God frowns upon revenge acts, and prayer is the best antidote for those twisted ideas that, if lived out, will eventually involve the court system.

I had never experienced the moment, however, when I didn't care about the messenger. The message was not at all about the words, but about how completely still I felt. The thunderstorm of grief had come, followed by the earthquake that shook down my life to the foundation, followed by a firestorm to burn off the excess. Now, I sat in the stillness of the fear and sorrow I felt.

Not anger, not wondering why, not even defending myself. I just

felt the stillness. And not the peaceful stillness, but the stillness
that follows the last skeletal breaths of someone who has fought
death for too long and I'm the only one in the room because the
family and friends are absent. The breath leaves the body, and I
am left alone with a corpse because I realize I didn't know anything about the person. The body is simply a container for a life I
never really knew.

When a relationship is trustworthy and honorable, we may
feel the initial jolt of betrayal and hurt upon hearing said uncomfortable news. I may initially want to get in my car and bust up
into my boyfriend's office and yell at him about the tramp he's
taken up with or call Mary and say, "So, I'm fat, am I?" But underneath that fear of possible hurt is the stillness that says, "Perhaps
before you have a scary crazy moment, you may want to consider
trusting the person because you know something about him or
her. You know their souls; trust that knowing."

Granted, our ever-expanding knowledge of the soul of another
may still end up with some tears and a few broken hearts, but the
hope is there that things can be resolved. And, usually after some
hesitantly awkward questions, I discover that his dinner date is his
best friend's daughter visiting the local college and that he shared
this information in the voicemail I received yesterday, but since I
was sure it was a reminder that the party started at 7:00, so please,
please, please be ready to go at 6:50 because I have a slight habit of
being late, I had just deleted it without listening.

Or I find that Mary was telling a friend I had gained weight
because for the last six months, I'd been on the trauma trim diet
and for once, gaining weight was a very, very good thing.

These people aren't containers; they are filled with a life, and
I know that life because it's intertwined with mine. I've heard
their stories, laughed with them, and been introduced to their
less than stellar qualities and they to mine. We've eaten too much
steak at Mr. John's and watched trashy television and had complex

discussions about health care and the impact of God's incarnation. And we are still friends. Truth in love is that earthy and real.

But in this moment, I had no hope that I could ask my boss if he really did want to fire me. I realized that I believed with every part of my fragile soul that whether he said everything that was attributed to him or he said nothing, speaking the truth in love was simply not on the table anymore.

The last breath left the body, and death settled in.

Death, again. I was getting very tired of her presence in my life. She accompanied me back to my office, where I got my purse, and walked out of the church where I had served not sure if I could ever walk back in. Maybe I should quit. Holy hell. How could this happen? That was the soundtrack in my head.

I breathed in. I wanted, again, for whatever magic to make all the discomfort go away. I knew that the corpse of what I had thought was a friendship would decay, and that would be unpleasant. And then some of that new wisdom appeared. I knew that the smell of decay isn't permanent, at least not for me. I could see the new light of resurrection. The shadows were still long and demanded most of the attention.

I turned over on my side and noticed my heart stayed put within my chest. Lady Death and I had become friends over the months. Her skeletal appearance didn't scare me . . . that much. She'd given me a bit of truth, that life always follows death, and usually in a way that is very unexpected.

That is, after all, the entirety of the message of Easter, that death is simply part of the cycle, but not the end. Death in her wisdom whispered again—that I was the child of a God who did not let death have the last word.

But who I was and whose I was—that voice I heard. I rolled my shoulders and stretched my joints as I burrowed under my comforter. I wiggled a bit and felt my backbone and my soul. Yep, they were most certainly connected.

And my heart was still beating strongly.

30

In Which We Meet Gabriel

MARY AND I WERE NOT lost, because I knew this beach well. A few more feet and there was a path that led to a hole in the wall that had the best steamed shrimp in the known world, in my opinion. We were on vacation and were committed to eating seafood at every meal. I had been coming to the Alabama coast for most of my life. When I stood in bare feet in the white Alabama sand, I remembered a quote I had seen on a postcard: "The cure for anything is saltwater—sweat, tears, or the sea." I had released enough of the tears. Summer in Alabama at the beach took care of the rest.

This evening, Mary and I sat on the porch of a place that looked more like a condemned building than a restaurant with a bottle of wine, some buckets of shrimp, and my computer. I was preparing my responses to the questions for St. Gabriel's, as well as two other churches that had recently asked me to enter their discernment process.

When a priest in the Episcopal Church enters into discernment to find a new church (or, as the rest of the world calls it, applies for a job), one of her first tasks is to answer questions posed by the church in question.

The questions St. Gabriel's posed all invited me to a deep level of authenticity. They asked what I liked best and least about my current position; how my experience would help them in their diversity of worship; how I would support their community diversity (they were an inclusive parish where all were welcomed); and how I could work with them with matters of spirituality and outreach. The question, however, that made my soul sing a few notes asked this: "What are your hopes and dreams as a priest, and how do you see serving our parish as advancing these?" They were asking me about my song, as a priest, and wondering how my song would sound with their song. I hadn't been asked that in years in the church.

Now I was fearful, because I had to claim my hopes and dreams. I had to say them aloud, not simply parrot someone else's or settle for what sounded good to others. I still felt fragile and awkward about answering these questions authentically instead of the things I was supposed to say. I was probably expected to say something about serving for years as an associate priest to gain experience to become a rector and how my experience would allow me to grow the church into a diocese unto itself.

I wrote about the church of my dreams being a place where we know we are loved by God, no matter what—in our joy and in our sadness, in our triumph and in our brokenness, that we are welcomed, honored, and heard where we are. I wrote about my joy in creating and celebrating beautiful, meaningful worship with and for the community that allowed us to celebrate and weep, sometimes during the same service, if needed. I wrote about my longing to lose our need to use externals like numbers and status to find our importance as the Body of Christ, instead asking ourselves if this church is a place where our fellow humans know that they have inherent dignity and that humans were created to flourish in that love and dignity.

In the hours and days of sun, restful sleep (yes, sleeping for the first time in months!), and far too much food, I answered questions posed by a church that I thought may be a place I could serve God. Where I could serve God, this self that I had been discovering who was not so interested in the clergy upward mobility or safety in numbers. Of course, seeking a parish based on expectations and assumptions or the sense of vocation as others had defined it is much easier. Nope, this place would need to be a place where my most authentic self would be welcomed in a diocese where my most authentic self would be welcomed.

Not that, at this time, I was even remotely clued in to the full aspects of this most authentic self. I was tentatively feeling the edges of my self and soul, newly exposed by God's gracious ripping away of the personas I had acquired. Reconstruction after deconstruction is a slow work of God, who never seems to be in any hurry to do much of anything in a speedy manner.

A truth about going through the woods with God is that when you start to come out on the other side, you are still healing. I could stand and wiggle my fingers. I could even do a few dance steps, but my joints where my soul was knit together were still tender. Doubt's voice was still mumbling words that were familiar, but no longer useful. Yet like the words of that bitter old aunt who would look at your new blue dress and say, "Oh, is that what you're going to wear?" the words still had power. They had the power to urge me back to that place where letting other people tell me what I wanted or needed was acceptable. They have the power to make you ignore the still, small voice of God for the loud, obnoxious voices of those who would rather you comply. They make you wonder, "What if?"

What if those voices that said I wasn't in a good place to hear another call were right? What if this place that felt wobbly but holy after so many months wasn't sustainable? What if this dress is a foolish mistake that will ensure I'll never have a date for the rest of my entire life?

I didn't wholly trust myself. I still gave air time to some voices from people that I would eventually evict from my life, but for now they were still living rent free in my soul. The journey to deep authenticity is not instantaneous, and it is exhausting. I knew there was a long to-do list, but I was also recognizing the efficacy of living one day, even one moment and task, at a time.

My recovery friends love to remind me that this is not new knowledge, but we hear what we hear when we need to hear it.

What I did feel sure of is that for the first time in months, maybe even a year, I felt stretched out in my skin, and this was my skin. Not anyone else's. So I answered the questions and sent them in.

Another truth about the discernment process is that it, like God, is not in any hurry. But I knew staying put was costly on many levels for me. I had listened to God and realized where I served was not where I was called to serve anymore. Listening to that voice was not casting aspersions on my current parish, any more than my liking college football better than college baseball denigrates the latter. Unfortunately, I felt from the clergy staff where I served that I had denigrated something of theirs.

We humans like to be on the popular end of the vote, perhaps. We like when we can all agree, when another's experience validates our own. I do, anyway. I feel comforted when I can assuage my fears and doubts by seeing that others are in line with me. I, however, had stepped out of line, and I felt the pressure of that retribution. I had to trust my voice, which was a new experience.

Thankfully, I had other voices to sing with me. Mary and Brad listened. My therapist offered insight and guidance, mostly by nudging me to trust my instincts and my own voice. I still marvel at the great courage and gift of that ability.

I still felt the church chipping away at my confidence when the rector told me he wanted my new parish to see how fabulous I was, and he didn't think I was there yet. I ignored him, and continued to get other invitations to apply for positions. My discernment at St. Gabriel's moved forward.

One Saturday afternoon I engaged in a telephone interview with the nominating committee of St. Gabriel's. I talked and listened. I listened to their questions and their responses, but mostly I listened to my heart. I listened for that part of my soul that would be moved not by logic, but by feeling.

One of the committee members asked me about coming from such a large parish, where we had hired help to set up chairs. They didn't have that at St. Gabriel's, and the committee wanted to know if that would be a challenge for me.

I told them about Greg.

Greg was a member of my first parish, and he struggled with alcoholism for years, especially during the first part of my tenure at Holy Name. One day his neighbors discovered him facedown in his front yard, almost dead. Between the effects of alcohol and exposure, he spent several weeks in the hospital before being moved into a retirement community. I worked with a wonderful social worker who, like me, realized Greg could not live on his own anymore. In his new home, he found sobriety and a life. He began visiting his fellow residents, bringing them newspapers and offering them his company. He became a faithful and sober member of Holy Name in his way. Decades of alcoholism has taken a toll. He appeared at the church regularly to help how he could, and often he and I would set up chairs for special events. As we would pull out chairs and line them up in neat rows, he recalled his life, often one of the same few stories he told over and over.

We set up chairs, and he told stories. Sometimes I listened. Other times I shook my head in frustration because I was setting up chairs and listening to the same story about his painting his car as a college student yet again. In the amazing, mundane, and frustrating, God is still present, even when it aggravates us.

Years later, in fact a few weeks before the retreat when I had spoken my deep truth in a graveyard, the then-rector at Holy

Name called with the news: Greg had terminal cancer and was expected to die in a matter of weeks. I thanked him for letting me know. He said he wasn't calling me to share the news, but he was calling to tell me Greg wanted me to preach at his funeral. Apparently, when asked why, he simply said, "She saved my life."

I'm not sure I did, actually. I don't think I did any more to save Greg's life from his alcoholism than Greg himself did. Salvation is not my charge; love is, and love is hard enough. I sat in the weight of the news of yet another death and the honor this man had offered me and thought about all the stories he told as we set up chairs over the course of years. Repetitive, mundane, even aggravating depending on how busy my day had been. But in those moments, I heard Greg. I could preach his funeral, and I could preach about a man I knew and loved, not simply a person whose story I would have to hear from his surviving family and friends. I could preach about my friend.

Greg's funeral was held in the parish hall because the church was undergoing renovations. I went for a quick trip soon after I'd returned from the beach. I helped set up the chairs for his funeral. I actually asked the sexton if I could finish setting up the chairs alone.

He looked at me quizzically.

"It helps me with my sermon," I explained.

He shrugged his shoulders and said yes. So I was alone, setting up the last dozen or so chairs for Greg's funeral. And with each chair, I heard Greg's stories. Again. And let Greg's life preach to me before I preached his funeral.

And this, I told St. Gabriel's, is why I wasn't bothered at all about setting up chairs in a parish. When I got to this part, I felt my heart squeeze a bit and the tears fell. The part of my soul who cared less about the resumé breathed deeply and nudged me a bit, telling me that that this may be the place God is calling you to serve. Not because they had the biggest budget or my first job would be to hire an associate (neither was true about St. Gabriel's), but because they asked me a question and the answer was about a small, mundane moment where God was present. Because they listened, and when I finished, held the space of silence for a moment before saying, "Thank you."

For the next six weeks, I waited.

Then, at the end of August, just at the academic year was getting started again at St. Paul's, I flew to Lexington to be interviewed as one of the three finalists to be considered for rector of St. Gabriel's.

31

Be Brave

OR A WHILE I FORGOT how to be brave.

Oh, I pretended to be brave. I told the truth when telling the truth was safe, or when telling the truth was a way to capitulate. Sometimes I didn't even tell the truth. I just smiled and stayed silent, or accepted other's truth as mine when it was really a lie in my soul. And I learned the cost of pretending to be brave was too high for me, so I retreated forward into brave authenticity.

My grandfather said Coach Bear Bryant, according to fact or legend or myth or the something in between that exists in the great stories in the South, told his quarterbacks to be brave before the game. God and Bear Bryant aren't all that distinct in parts of my birth state of Alabama. After all the offensive schemes and defensive tactics had been reviewed one last time. After all the last-minute reminders of which players from Georgia or Florida or Auburn to watch. After Coach Bryant, in his deep voice, said whatever words he knew would motivate his players to push themselves to the edge of love for the holy sport of Alabama and then go three more steps, because victory rests in the beyond. After those moments, he looked his quarterback in the eyes, rested the weight of his hands and a grand tradition on a boy's shoulders, and said, "Be brave."

Bravery is the willingness to give space to the courage and fear within each of us that always exist in our souls together. Our fearful soul entices us to grasp for titles and awards, those external validations that, when we doubt our worth, we can point to and think, "Well, I must be a good person because I have all these things to prove my importance." Our fearful souls yearn for control. Brave souls know when stripped bare with our scars fully visible, we are worthy of love and dignity in that scarred nakedness. No titles, no salary increases, no trappings of power, just our very selves and souls.

Bravery is hard work that involves stripping away the pretty to see the dirt on our souls. The first football coach I ever knew, my grandfather, said no player in football should leave with a clean uniform. He would say that. The man who served in the Pacific theater in World War II as a minesweeper; who was prepared to be a part of the first wave of the invasion of Japan, with 100 percent casualties predicted; who was a football player and coach and high school principal who integrated his high school by reminding local racists that he was a good shot and unafraid to use a gun, would recognize that if you're not in the dirt and getting it rubbed in your clothes and face and soul, you aren't being brave. If you aren't chancing victory because you're too busy calculating the price, you aren't being brave.

Because bravery hurts. It comes at a cost. Somewhere in a room or a side street or on the shores of a body of water, Jesus looked at those who would follow him and said, "Be brave."

And someone asked, "Why? Don't we just have to love each other, be merciful, and forgive?"

Jesus nodded and said what all those who have lived with bravery know: it will hurt, you will not always like it, and there will be blood.

While we in the South love to relate sports analogies to life, even to religion, in the end, sports are sports, not life. Football, baseball, basketball—they are all entertainment, and they are all optional. Plenty of people live their entire lives quite fully never having stepped on the gridiron or the hardwood or the diamond. Life, however, is not optional. We are all required to participate. We are not always brave. I had discovered that plenty of people live their entire lives without being brave.

I had lived my life for the past few years without being brave. I had appeased my rector in the church by agreeing with him, even excusing words that violated and bullied me. When I reached out for help from his superiors, I was told, "Lots of people say they are bullied. Good luck with your job search." They would be brave from the sidelines and hope the best for me, but they were not about to get their uniforms dirty while I bled from the wounds.

In my desire to be safe, I had believed others in the church could make me safe. They could not. Safety for me came with the courage to rediscover that part of me that felt with courage her emotions—sadness, joy, grief, and fear. I had touched my wounds and felt them not just as places where my soul had been cut, but also as places God could shine through. And I felt brave when I decided—I decided—to listen to where God was calling me and trust that voice instead of the voices of those who aren't brave, but would talk as if they were, telling me what they would do if they were living my life. I also knew that being brave meant facing the deep truth that even at my best, my very best, I will bleed and weep because of living life.

I felt brave again, until I sat in the bishop's office in the diocese of Lexington.

I arrived to make an official visit to St. Gabriel's, to see if we might have a ministry together. The days were hectic and busy. Actual on the ground interviews with a parish are not vacation weekends. You and they are trying to see as much of each other as you can in a limited amount of time. You eat meals with members of the parish, listening to each other, asking questions. Over three days, I met members of the parish and toured Lexington and felt generally overwhelmed. I met more people than I thought were in the entire Episcopal Church. Everyone asked questions. I asked questions. Sometimes I had answers; sometimes I just said, "I don't know, but I'd like us to find out together."

I met Kathryn face to face. We embraced like two women who had known each other for years. We made plans for dinner on my last night in Lexington, so I could process my visit with her. And then I met with the bishop. He smiled when I walked into his office. Kathryn assured me all would be well, but my experience with clergy over the last year left me guarded and fearful of what knives they hid behind their backs as they shook my hand and said we were all friends.

We exchanged a few pleasantries. He asked me about my visit so far. I told him it felt like sorority rush on steroids. He laughed. We talked generally about the diocese of Lexington and St. Gabriel's. I relaxed inch by inch, until he asked, "Tell me about what is going on between you and the rector at St. Paul's."

I felt the initial stir to diminish what had happened, to excuse everything to personality differences or a mistake on my part or anything but my bare naked truth. I wanted to change the topic. I wanted to lose the ability to speak.

And then I remembered God's whisper, "Be brave."

So I told the bishop of Lexington my story. I told him how I had gone to St. Paul's for reasons that were more about thinking it was what I was supposed to do that what I was called to do, but that somehow God was still present. There were things about my ministry there I loved. I told him how I had started the Bad Girls Book Club for women to gather and read seemingly secular books for their spiritual messages. I told him how I had participated with other area ministers to be publicly tested for HIV/AIDS to encourage more people to be tested. I told him of the people I had come to love and would miss at St. Paul's.

Then, I took a deep breath. "I was called into the rector's office a few weeks ago. I felt like I was being called into the principal's office. I knew I was going in to offer up my pound of flesh for not being one of the gang."

The Bishop sat quietly, his hands folded over his chin.

"I sat across from his desk and listened to his litany of all the things I had done wrong, all the mistakes I had made, and all the ways I had hurt him. Some of them were valid. My text message one Sunday that I wouldn't be at church was passive-aggressive. But being late to his last-minute dinner party? I'd been talking to my mother about my stepfather's surgery. I felt like he listed my faults, shortcomings, and defects just to hurt me.

"But I sat there, and I listened to his truth, and it was painful for me. I hoped he'd give me a chance to speak my truth, that I felt smothered by the expectations of the rector. I wanted to say that I felt intimidated, harassed, and bullied by his words and actions; how I understood that he wanted to fire me, and when I asked his superior for help, I was told he would help me leave and hopefully I could 'work it out' before I left.

"He told me instead, 'Don't ever hurt me like that again.' Then he just said he was sorry for anything he'd done that might have hurt me, and I knew, without a doubt, that any respect, loyalty, and trust I had for him was gone."

I breathed deeply again and fiddled with the button on my green blazer. "I apologized, because I need insurance and a job. I am sorry for some things, but I really just wanted to get out of that office before any more of my soul was devoured."

I didn't truly feel sorry for all I had done that hurt the rector. I was sorry for some of the things I'd done. I was sorry that I couldn't live up to his expectations, that I had failed at whatever role I was hired to play in his life. I was sorry that I did not feel grace in the room at the moment, but a clear distinction of power, and I was the underling, the kid sister, who was to be scolded.

The bishop sat for a moment. "Maybe he wasn't sorry for anything he'd done."

I nodded, "And that hurts even more." My eyes were tearing. I breathed deeply, and found the bravery to say one final thing with every note of truth I had in my soul. "The church broke my heart."

And then I stopped speaking, feeling quite wobbly and quite sure this bishop would not want someone like me to be a priest in his diocese. Wobbly as I felt, I knew I had been brave to speak my truth. It hurt, I did not like it, and I was waiting for the blood.

Instead, he said those magical words of love and healing.

"I'm sorry."

Magical because they recognized the injury. Loving because they weren't a flippant or thin blanket apology that isn't really sorry for anything. He, as a bishop who gets to wear that interesting shade of amethyst, spoke for the church, the church saying, "I'm sorry for what we have done to break your heart. What do we do now?"

What now for me was recognizing that I was surviving a situation where my soul had been broken and beaten by those who vowed to love and serve as Christ loved and served. What now for me was standing in my wobbliness and knowing that I was healing, and this moment in the bishop's office was yet one more moment of salve. What now was a hope that I might be called to this diocese and serve with a bishop who believed broken hearts and crucified souls that have experienced resurrection are useful, even valuable, in ministry.

I wanted to fall back in love with the church. I wanted to remember why I do love the church, my ministry, and the people I serve.

32

Walking in Bare Feet

I SAT IN THE DARK.

At my final night of interviews, after all the voices told me that I was not in a place to enter the search process, that the parish I was visiting wasn't big enough or rich enough or something enough for me, or that there was a list of things I should pay attention to when I did the official visit, which did not include the still small voice, I felt overwhelmed and exhausted.

And I kept listening for that moment, that feeling that was illogical and overwhelming. That feeling that said, "Yes!" to this place.

A caveat is that I also realized my soul may sing in this place, but the church may have other ideas. There were other candidates to interview. My soul may say, "Yes," but theirs may say, "No."

Such is the stuff of faith.

After a three-hour interview one night with the entire search committee that asked all sorts of questions, I felt exhausted. I asked Frank, the person who drove me, if I could have some time alone in the church. He said, "Of course."

So I went alone into the church. I started to turn on the lights, but decided to leave the darkness. I looked at the images of God in this space. Open air, clear windows, a simple cross, and a frieze of a young mother cradling a fat baby to her breast. In this place, God had not been relegated to images of white men. She was young. He was a round infant. And God was the building itself, open and fluid, rising upward and grounding downward in pale wood walls and grey, red, and brown slate tiles.

I sat on the front pew and wondered. I wondered what, exactly, I should feel. I had a few moments where I thought logic was a fine thing to use, exclusively. Could I pray in here? Could I preach in here? Did I like the space?

I sat in the dark. And then I began to cry. One sure way to know that you are sitting firmly in your feelings is through tears. My tears are the ultimate speakers of truth. They appear when my words are too limiting to express my soul, so they simply speak their own language. And suddenly, whether I could pray or preach or if I liked the space didn't matter, because my soul felt familiar and safe enough with this space to weep.

My soul whispered, "Walk the perimeter. In bare feet," so I took off my shoes and walked the entire perimeter of the church. My bare feet touched each stone that surrounded the center. I pointed my feet with each step, an elegant and earthy dance around sacred space. My toes nudged the space where slate floor and wooden walls met. Somewhere, the priestly matriarchs of eons past murmured their primeval chants of prayer to match the pace of my steps. I walked until I reached the altar, where I lit the candles. Real wax candles, I noticed. They would burn down with each lighting. They would show their use. St. Paul's and many other churches use liquid wax candles on their altars. I don't like them; they never show their use. They always look perfect on the outside, while the liquid fuel inside is consumed away from view.

I stood in bare feet and smudged mascara and wondered for a moment what to do next. Until I opened my mouth and began to sing parts of the Eucharist. The sound of my voice filled the space, danced on the stone floors, joined the mothers of the ages, and came back to my soul. I could sing here.

And in that very holy moment, I knew God was calling me to be the rector of St. Gabriel's.

Knowing something in your soul does not equate with immediate resolution. God did not seem to insert that into creation. I was the first candidate that St. Gabriel's interviewed, so I had to wait several weeks until they made a decision.

Several l-o-n-g weeks.

And I was still in the search process with other parishes. Sort of like dating other men when you know you've already met the one that fills your soul like no other. But logic does have its uses, and one of them is staying in the process until it's complete, just to make sure. So in between keeping my head down at my current parish to avoid any more wounds to my soul and interviews with other parishes and thankfully two conferences scheduled that filled up my time with wonderful people, I waited.

I am not particularly gifted at waiting. I had learned on this journey that God is busy, even when I feel like I'm doing nothing. The imperceptible movement of star dust before the Big Bang created a new reality. That is holy waiting. But waiting I was, until God called forth the moment of incarnation, when the new thing that I had suffered and struggled through for years, could finally be born and my world would change.

Life should be easy and tidy and fair. Somewhere, I recognized that lie as truth. And when life is not easy and tidy and fair, my immediate reaction was that something was wrong. In the past years, I had discovered life is hard and messy and unfair and miraculous and filled with love. One would think after living through and serving as a chaplain at Ground Zero and through Hurricane Katrina, I would have figured out that lesson. And I had, intellectually. In my mind I understood those truths and could preach on them and write on them very well. Life is hard, thus the whole Good Friday bit. Nicest guy on earth gets handed over to die a rather unpleasant death. Yep, life is hard and messy and unfair. But then—yippee! Easter Sunday comes and makes all that mess better.

Life, I was discovering, is lived without knowing the details of the ending. I know that love wins. That much I knew—in my head. But when my heart felt like it was falling out of my soul so much so that I slept on my stomach to ease the pain, I was not so sure. The past years had been a descent into death and darkness.

I had no idea about what being a rector may entail. I knew it would not be safe, and for the first time in my life, I was able to speak that truth. But I would be safe in another way, because I had learned to speak my truth.

I had returned to my mother's house after attending a conference. The night-blooming jasmine made sitting on the porch swing reading about the latest celebrity divorce a holy moment. I breathed in deeply, and the phone rang. It was a Lexington, Kentucky, phone number.

I answered. The entire search committee and vestry were on the other end. One person asked me, "Would you like to be our next rector?"

And, as I pushed the porch swing back and forth with my bare feet, I smiled and said, "I have been waiting for you for a long time."

33

Holy Week, Again

W E BEGAN THE EASTER VIGIL outside in the courtyard. The parishioners of St. Gabriel's gathered in
the waning light of Holy Saturday. I'd found some
beautiful vestments in the attic of the diocesan office and bor-
rowed them for this service. I prayed the opening prayer, facing
the stack of wood in an outdoor fire pit.

> Dear friends in Christ: On this most holy night,
> in which our Lord Jesus passed over from death
> to life, the Church invites her members, dis-
> persed throughout the world, to gather in vigil
> and prayer. For this is the Passover of the Lord,
> in which, by hearing his Word and celebrating his
> Sacraments, we share in his victory over death.

One of the parishioners assisting me handed me a match.
I touched it to the wood, and it caught quickly. Using the old
healing oil that someone was ready to throw out as a fire-starter
had worked well. On the afternoon of Palm Sunday, I had refur-
bished a Paschal Candle I'd found in the basement. It had been
used years ago, then stored away. In my weekly exploration of the

nooks and crannies of my new parish, I'd discovered it with the help of another parishioner. With a good rubbing and some acrylic paint, the real-wax candle was reborn with color and shine. I took the Paschal Candle and lit it from the fire. Wax dripped into the fire and sizzled. We then put incense in the thurible. The sun set. The Paschal Candle flickered. The smell of rich incense filled the courtyard. And we prayed. Then the light of Christ, symbolized by this found candle, a bit used but still beautiful, led us into the church.

There, I sang the Exsultet. And for the first time in my entire experience of singing that ancient hymn, I didn't miss a note. We listened to the savings acts of God as revealed in scripture. We sang. And when I stood in front of the altar, watching parishioners clutch bells in anticipation, I paused just a moment to wait, to savor this profound moment.

I wanted to see the darkness and the light that would not be overcome by the darkness. I wanted to embrace in my soul the darkness I had journeyed through, and the light that I rediscovered. I wanted to be overwhelmed by the feeling that I was falling back in love with the Church . . . and falling in love with my messy, authentic self, as well. I took a deep breath and smiled, then said, bravely and joyfully, "Alleluia! Christ is risen!"

The lights came on, the flowers came out, and the altar was vested for Easter. Bells rang, people sang, and we greeted the resurrection.

Following the service, we had a reception, complete with champagne. I left my shoes in my office and padded around the parish hall in bare feet, talking with people about all manner of things. As people eased home, I said goodbye to them, then went into my office to ready for tomorrow's services.

I thought about how much my life had changed in one year. Actually in four years. My story of grief, a broken heart, pain, and life reminded me that resurrection wasn't just a story in the Gospels. I had died and lived it. My path was mine. The scars were mine. The redemption was God's. No one could save me or make me safe, I had learned. God and I were the heroines of our story. I learned that living for someone else's agenda and expectations and needs, even when they sounded important and logical, almost killed my soul. Maybe for a time, it did kill most of my soul.

So I wandered, and with the help of friends and God, I found my way to my naked, authentic, wobbly soul. I even learned that I do my best work in bare feet, a lesson I learned at great cost. I grieve that many don't ever open themselves to that lesson. I also want to drink a shot of bourbon at the knowledge that once you open your soul to the great events that must be outgrown, God stays with you, offering you more ways to grow.

Great. Just great.

And I will be here, listening to that feeling of God moving in my soul. Crying when I need to cry, which I do with great abandon now. Laughing at my foolishness. Feeling my gut. Drawing with my left hand. And standing in bare feet.

A parishioner knocked on my office door. I looked up.

Frank, the chair of the nominating committee that called me here, smiled at me. "Just want to tell you we're the last ones leaving. We've locked up."

"Thanks," I said, and waved as he and his wife walked out of my office.

I walked into the church. Votives flickered on the Marian altar. I started to turn on the lights, but instead walked to the chairs in the front and sat in front of the altarpiece of Mary gently holding her baby Jesus to her face.

In the quiet darkness, I sat, listening to the comforting silence. I breathed in deeply; I could still smell the sweet incense that lingered from the Vigil. I started to say a verbal prayer, but decided simply to feel a prayer. I felt my broken places, the cuts and mutilations, the scars and wounds, and I honored them, even found the love to be thankful for who I had become because of them. I felt anger, still, for those who had inflicted some of the wounds, and I knew the journey of forgiveness rested in my future. I felt my soul sing and dance. I even felt the cool slate floor beneath my tired feet. My toes ran over the smooth stones. I quietly sang my favorite part of the Exsultet again.

> How wonderful and beyond our knowing, O God, is your mercy and loving-kindness to us, that to redeem a slave, you gave a Son.
>
> How holy is this night, when wickedness is put to flight, and sin is washed away. It restores innocence to the fallen, and joy to those who mourn. It casts out pride and hatred, and brings peace and concord.
>
> How blessed is this night, when earth and heaven are joined and man is reconciled to God.

In the dark, I felt safe. Tears of grief, joy, brave hope, and insane faith slipped down my cheeks. And here, in this space, I simply let them fall. I would return to this holy space tomorrow to celebrate new life in Christ and new life in me.

Night is dark, and I am finally home.

Acknowledgments

I DEAS BORNE FROM A NEW Year's Eve party in the French Quarter during a conversation with a drag queen in a full-length bejeweled gown and a man in a tuxedo with an affected and probably fake British accent are almost always trouble.

"We should write a blog," Laurie suggested, topping off our champagne. The drag queen squealed with delight, and the maybe-British man from southern Louisiana said, "I have the perfect title. Dirty Sexy Ministry."

Mary rolled her eyes, still annoyed at the faux British accent. But somewhere between toasting the New Year and our New Year's Day lunch over biscuits and sweet tea at Cracker Barrel the next day, we created a blog. Not to worry, we both thought. Who would want to read about our misdeeds besides us? The stories were funny to us, but would anyone else think so?

Our original aim was humor in ministry and the church. We enjoyed pointing out strange moments in this interesting life of the priesthood. As we kept writing about our ministry, our faith, and our church, one theme ran through many of our blog posts: grief.

That the church, which is supposed to be a place to bind up broken hearts, could be just as uncomfortable and awkward with grief as every other human institution was shocking to us. And we wrote about that shock and that pain. We began receiving e-mails from people who resonated with our essays. And some wondered if we would write a book.

Really? A book? We never thought that what we were writing on the blog would lead to a book, but here we are, and here is our book. The names of the parishes have been changed, as have some of the names and identifying information of the people and places.

During a conversation with one of the people who appears in this book, we asked if she wanted to read the chapter in which she appears.

"No, it's your truth. Just because I might not remember or have experienced it in just the way you did doesn't make your truth or mine any less, well, true."

Writing about difficult and painful situations that involve other people is never easy. This is our truth, how we experienced these situations and how we felt. Others may have experienced a different truth. Life in a community of respectful love is not about selecting the "right" truth, but having space and courage to hear everyone's truth in their experiences and stories. Telling our stories about grief and about joy was challenging and painful. Reliving heartache is never fun. We both thought that we were done with grief, but grief was not done with us, and never will be. But we also got to remember the joy and laughter. Perhaps we thought, at our darkest times, that we were done with joy, but joy is not done with us either.

None of this would be possible without the readers and followers of our blog, Dirty Sexy Ministry. Your support, comments, e-mails, and expressions of friendship let us know that we are not alone on this wonderful and slightly twisted journey of vocation, service to God, and life. Thank you, thank you, thank you from our broken, scarred, and joyful hearts.

Thank you to our families who instilled in both of us a love of writing and reading and a healthy amount of crazy. In a good way.

Thank you to those friends who have known and loved us through stupidity and wisdom and laughter and tears: to Emma (mommy loves you), Bradley C., Susan McD., Amy, Elise, Kay, Jim, Joseph, Sumor, Susan W., Amy D., Connie, the General Seminary Alpha Females, and the BECWs. We love you. You are our persons. You would have the shovel ready, and we would do the same.

Thank you to the parishes that have loved and nurtured us throughout our faith journeys, both as lay and ordained women, especially our current parishes, St. Michael the Archangel in Lexington, Kentucky, and The Episcopal Church of the Good Shepherd in Austin, Texas. We are grateful, especially, to the clergy who have mentored us through the years: The Rev. Ben Alford, The Rev. Morgan Allen, The Rev. Tom Cook, The Rev. Gedge Gayle, The Rt. Rev. Charles Jenkins, The Rev. S. Albert Kennington, and The Rt. Rev. Stacy Sauls.

Thank you to Nancy Bryan, who managed to read perhaps the most disorganized book proposal ever and still see something worth pursuing, and to our editor Lauren Winner, who took one look at our original manuscript and said, "You can do better. Tell your truth." She was right.

Thank you to the random things in life that keep us grounded: Diamond View Farms where Laurie rides (and occasionally falls off) horses, good chocolate, Law and Order: SVU marathons, Frank and Jutta, Twitter conversations during late-night writing sessions, coffee with chicory, Cracker Barrel, and the deep, deep truth that resurrection always follows death. Somehow. Someway.

Thanks be to God.

Discussion Questions
by Lauren Winner

Introduction

1. Do you think of priests or other ministers as being beautiful messes?

2. What do you hear God saying to you about your own beautiful messiness?

Chapter 1: Almost Dying Sucks . . . Joy

1. Have you ever had an experience of your love or hope or joy dying? What choices were available to you, and what did you choose?

Chapter 2: Going Home

1. Mary describes New Orleans as a place that held real meaning for her. What place—a building, a neighborhood, a city—holds the most meaning for you?

2. In this chapter, we begin to get a sense of Mary and Laurie's friendship, and why it was important for the two women. What friendships have most sustained you?

Chapter 3: RESPECT

1. Mary writes "I thought the rules were if you are a good and kind person, people will like and respect you." What do you think "the rules" are? Have you ever found yourself in a situation where the rules you took for granted seemed not to hold? What did you do?

Chapter 4: The Dark Night of the Soul Is Not Romantic at All

1. What is your experience of nighttime? Is it the hardest time of the day?

2. What feelings do the phrase "dark night of the soul" provoke in you?

Chapter 5: Six

1. In this chapter, Mary describes endurance and hope. What experience in your life required the most endurance? Where did you find hope?

Chapter 6: Strong and Faithful, and Broken

1. When have you encountered Jesus in the midst of your own vulnerability?

2. Have you experienced a loss that made you a better minister, or a better disciple of Jesus?

Chapter 7: To Cope or to Heal

1. "Healing meant that I needed to learn to swim in rough waters," writes Mary. What are the rough waters in which you have had to swim in order to find healing? Who was there swimming with you?

Chapter 8: Grinding Coffee

1. How has God participated in the easy but fulfilling relationships in your life? How has God participated in the hard and challenging relationships?

Chapter 9: Divorce

1. When a relationship ends (marriage, friendship, or job, for example), have you found reflecting on your responsibility in the failure helpful or hurtful to your healing?

Chapter 10: Put Her Down

1. Imagine yourself having a conversation with Jesus, across your kitchen table, or while driving to work. What would you talk about? What do you want to say to Jesus? What do you imagine Jesus saying to you?

Chapter 11: A Miracle of Love Will Take Away Your Pain . . .

1. Do you look for joy and happiness within yourself, or do you find it in someone else near to you?

2. Mary's daughter came to her right after her marriage ended. Have you ever experienced a loss and a blessing in such rapid succession? What did the loss and the blessing have to do with one another? How did it feel to have the loss and the abundance so close, cheek-by-jowl?

Chapter 12: Creating a Crisis

1. In your life, what is the relationship between God's agency and your agency, God's control and your actions?

2. Have you ever created a crisis for yourself? Why? What happened?

3. How is your identity, your sense of yourself, vested in your job? How is your identity vested in your place in a church or other spiritual community?

Chapter 13: Anger and Free Time

1. Mary and Laurie both discuss their fear of getting angry, yet expressing their anger helps them both heal and move forward. Why are we fearful of anger? How has God used, or how can God use, anger in your spiritual life?

Chapter 14: Getting Yes in a No World

1. Do you live like you have been resurrected? If not, what would it look like to live that way?

Chapter 15: At Last

1. Have you ever needed to let any old assumptions or old habits die, so that you might be open to new life? What did you need to let die? Did you grieve the death? What new life was born?

Chapter 16: New Plan: Listen to What God Says

1. How does it feel to imagine adopting as your mantra "New Plan: Listen to What God Says"?

Chapter 17: Pulling at Threads

1. Can you recall a time when you thought you were undertaking something small, something simple . . . and it turned out to be an experience of pulling at a thread? What were the unexpected results of tugging at that thread?

Chapter 18: Bleeding, Leaving, and Crying

1. In this chapter, Laurie interprets her experience with reference to the biblical prophet Jeremiah. What biblical character do you think best interprets your spiritual life, right now?

2. Do you feel safe or unsafe in church? Why?

Chapter 19: Fine, Except I hurt

1. What are your thoughts about what Laurie called "the mind-body-spirit connection"? How is your physical well-being connected to your emotional or spiritual well-being?

Chapter 20: Filled with Heaviness

1. What are your experiences of being near, even touching, dead bodies?

2. Laurie invokes the Celtic concept of being in a "thin place." What is a thin place? When were you most recently in a thin place, and how did you carry that experience with you into the rest of life?

Chapter 21: Grandmother

1. Laurie writes of her final visit with her grandmother, "I told her I loved her, kissed her again, and walked out for what we both knew would be the final time we would see each other on this side of the kingdom." Have you visited with someone for a final time? What were your feelings? What did you say? What do you wish you had said or even left unsaid?

2. Do Laurie's feelings of resentment at being present with parishioners during their deaths but not being able to be present for her own loved one's deaths surprise you?

Chapter 22: Lost

1. Have you ever been called to go to Nineveh?

2. Has God ever allowed you to be swallowed whole? What happened next?

Chapter 23: Amid the Encircling Gloom

1. Where is your encircling gloom? When you've been in the midst of it, have you had a sense of God leading you on?

Chapter 24: The Zombie of God

1. Have you had an experience of God coaxing you into death so that you can return to life?

2. What does it mean to be lost in the deep of God? How is this similar and different to Mary's experience of the "dark night of the soul"?

Chapter 25: Drawing into Grief

1. Both Mary and Laurie recount seeing therapists who ask them wise questions and listen to them well. Who are the people who have played this role in your life? How did you find those people, and how did you carry their questions and their listening into the rest of your life?

2. What if you tried to draw your grief or sorrow with your nondominant hand? After doing so, describe your experience, your feelings, and perhaps what you drew.

Chapter 26: Holy Week

1. How do you respond to Laurie's statement that "waiting is part of God's holiness"?

2. Where do you do your best crying?

Chapter 27: Broken Truth Found in the Graveyard

1. Have you ever gone on a retreat? What happened? Whom did you meet while there?

2. Imagine going on a retreat next week: what would you be seeking?

Chapter 28: I Am Wobbly and Alive

1. Laurie describes sacrificing huge parts of herself to "gods of comfort and the agenda of others and simply not rocking the boat." What gods have you sacrificed parts of yourself to?

2. What song has God given you?

Chapter 29: Death at a Parish

1. How do you respond when someone tells you something you don't want to hear—something like your ex-boyfriend's new girlfriend is so sweet and cute? Can gossip remind you of God?

2. When have you sat in stillness?

Chapter 30: In Which We Meet Gabriel

1. When have you been asked questions that have demanded authenticity of you? When have you asked such questions to someone else?

2. How can you compare Laurie's interview and experience with St. Gabriel's with her interview with St. Paul's?

Chapter 31: Be Brave

1. Have you ever forgotten to be brave? How did you make a return to bravery?

2. Have you fallen in and out of love with the church? Or in and out and in again?

Chapter 32: Walking in Bare Feet

1. Why was it important for Laurie to walk in bare feet? What experience in your own life did her bare feet story remind you of?

Chapter 33: Holy Week, Again

1. Describe a time when you experienced resurrection.

2. Laurie's experience of darkness is much different in this moment (compared to the chapel in Spain). How can darkness become a meaningful part of our souls and our faith instead of something of which we are fearful?

CPSIA information can be obtained at www.ICGtesting.com
Printed in the USA
LVOW081215220113

316712LV00001B/4/P